UNPRINCIPLED

**A High School Principal's Story of Addiction,
Downfall, and Recovery**

Patrick V. Farley, M. Ed

Foreword by Dr. Angela Olerich, D.O.

Edited by Melissa Brock

Design by Erik Hoveland

Marketing Consultant: Rodney Hatfield

*Unprincipled: A High School Principal's
Story of Addiction, Downfall, and Recovery*
Paperback ISBN 979-8-9939930-0-3
Hardcover ISBN 979-8-9939930-1-0

For Cakes

This book is also dedicated to my friend John Osboe, whose kindness and character left a lasting mark on my life and the lives of many others.

Contents

"The only way out is through."

—Robert Frost

Foreword

As a family medicine physician in the rural Midwest, I have the privilege of being involved in some of the most transformative moments in people's lives. These moments can be celebratory, marking great achievements, or they can be deeply challenging, representing some of the most difficult times individuals may face. Alcohol use disorder (AUD) and addiction are not immune to this discussion.

Over the years, I've had the pleasure of getting to know the Farley family. The connection to Pat, his wife, kids, and support system is why I appreciate his remarkable story and perspective.

On both a personal and professional level, it's been an honor to be along the journey as Pat reclaimed agency over something so incredibly difficult. Addiction is an area where successful escape is not so common. I've witnessed many patients succumb to alcohol-related liver disease; consequences include ascites (recurrent fluid accumulation) as they fight against the inevitable. I have also seen patients lose their hard-fought battles to addiction and mental health by suicide, and to overdose-related complications. Therefore, when Pat was able to regain control over addiction, it was not simply a mental feat. Addiction is physical, neurological, emotional, and very real. Its grip is often cruel, unwavering, and relentless. Sadly, successful recovery is not something I see often. The vulnerability Pat showed in confiding his struggles with me is a privilege I don't take lightly.

All too frequently, I witness the significant stigma surrounding AUD and other addictions. This often makes it incredibly difficult for people to seek support, achieve success, and maintain sobriety. Fear of judgment and shame are massive hurdles to seeking care. The next barrier represents the ongoing maintenance of leveraging continual control over addiction. Relapse rates are high, and I suspect the reasons are multifaceted. One of the most momentous challenges is access to care. It's expensive, treatment centers are hard to find (and even if you find one) it's a matter of matching the right program or mentor to your needs. Compounding the problem, individuals are still trying to navigate the pressures of work, securing employment, and maintaining family relationships. The complexity of these factors creates an environment where success can feel out of reach, despite the deep desire for change.

Ingrained, uninformed societal stigma certainly does not help. Understanding the more complex underlying issues of addiction is key: genetics, past trauma, neurobiology, adverse childhood events, mental health, etc.

A significant asset in this book is the author's deep understanding of psychology, neural wiring, and addiction. He's incredibly well-educated, which, in many ways, can make overcoming addiction even more challenging. When one knows a great deal about the science behind addiction psychology, it can often lead to individuals over-intellectualizing the struggle. Their own thinking can generate seemingly valid and even academic anchored excuses in defense of the addiction. That's what makes this book so powerful.

Unprincipled offers an honest look at the various aspects of the mind that may grapple with addiction while also providing a guide of sorts toward sobriety and recovery. Pat is in a uniquely qualified position to share not only personal anecdotes, but also to offer insights and lay the groundwork to understand the underlying pathophysiology of addiction, the neural wiring/misfirings, and how the two are intimately intertwined. Understanding the brain connection and bringing awareness to it, are paramount in destigmatizing addiction to the general public.

Professionally, I can explain the neurobiological adaptations and changes that occur with AUD, but the personal battle is something that transcends science. It's the deeply human experience that he conveys through these pages.

I believe his story will serve as an invaluable guide for anyone who has struggled with addiction or has witnessed a loved one fight this life long battle. It provides a perspective that's hard to grasp unless you've experienced it firsthand. This is a feature of which neurobiology alone can't fully capture.

Dr. Angela Olerich, D.O.

Preface

Most stories follow a journey, and mine, through the chaos of alcohol addiction, was no exception. It was a path I didn't walk so much as crawl, bruised by its pain and complexity. This is my story of a dormant monster I awakened, fed to great livelihood, and allowed to become all-powerful.

Writing this book felt excruciating. It was difficult to find the words and also challenging to convey just how hopeless one feels while trapped in the throes of addiction. Every brave soul who has fought addiction has their own unique tale to tell, but I'm confident I'm a statistic. Many would shy away from this way of thinking, but many of the markers are there: divorced parents in early adolescence, a history of abuse, difficulty adjusting in school, an alcoholic stepfather. I have a genetic predisposition to addiction, many in my family have grown to know the struggle. How could I *not* become an alcoholic?

It's easy to assign this and other words of proverbial wisdom to explain my descent: "The apple doesn't fall far from the tree."

I played the most significant role in what became this mess. Yet, *I did not want this. Nobody does.* I studied addiction academically in my twenties and passionately taught addiction prevention and psychology classes. I was aware of its operation and progressions, curious and intrigued by its neuroscience. And yet here we are.

I wish it were as simple as proverbs and theories. I wish this mess was clean and simple instead of the complicated fog in which addiction manifests itself.

My addiction cost me my career, and worse, I bestowed incredible pain on my friends, family, students, faculty, and the staff at the high school where I worked.

Unfortunately, the collective societal opinion regarding alcoholism or alcohol use disorder still prevails: Alcoholics are indolent people with a lack of willpower and zero work ethic who possess no real strength or moral compass. We are low, shameful, *unprincipled* . . . drunks.

In his book *Man's Search for Meaning*, Viktor Frankl suggests "that to live is to suffer." To live well or to have a chance at finding happiness, we must make sense of our suffering. This book is my attempt to do just that. I have no illusions that I've suffered more than others. I'm not unique in my suffering. We all experience hardship and difficulty. My struggles are probably not any greater than yours. Though I've come to learn that no matter what we've endured, with empathy and understanding, we may find our own purpose. Perhaps it is pain and suffering that leads many of us to track down that all-too-elusive pursuit of happiness. I believe *you* (as millions of us have done) can create a new life, free of alcohol and find a new life if addiction has you.

I'm not trying to seek pity or suggest my life has been worse than most, I've been fortunate to have had so many people that have shown me love in my life. I hope to simply tell my story and teach a few lessons that led me toward recovery. I hope to turn my mess into a message (I have the heart of a teacher, after all!).

I'm also not striving to convince society to cease alcohol consumption, nor shame or one-up those who choose to imbibe. Millions enjoy alcohol in moderation, others choose to leave it alone. However, like me, there are those who go on to develop a real problem with alcohol. It is to the latter group that I write on behalf of here.

I hope to inspire you if you have a problem with alcohol with one main message: *There is hope. There is a way out.* If not, perhaps you may find some meaning in your own journey.

Best wishes to you all as you proceed through the pages of my story.

Chapter 1

The Weight of Nothingness

"Your worst sin is that you destroyed and betrayed
yourself for nothing."

—Fyodor Dostoevsky

Friday, December 8, the day they found me
drinking on the job as assistant principal of my
school district, was overcast with a hint of sun,
but the air felt balmy. Late autumn winds and
rain over the past few weeks had dismantled
the colorful fall foliage, and I glimpsed barren,
brown neighborhood lawns through the truck's
passenger window. Watching the umber lawns
pass one by one, *blip, blip, blip*, made me sick
to my stomach, and I slid my eyes toward the
driver and wished with all my heart that *he*
wasn't sitting in the driver's seat.

Normally, I would have reveled in the
unexpected reprieve from the notoriously cold
Iowa weather, but the morning felt like it
should have been a normal frigid December
day—I felt as if there was a block of ice sitting
in my chest.

I was in no shape to drive.

Matt, my boss, the school superintendent
who had caught wind that I had been drinking
at work, gripped the steering wheel of his ruby

Ford F-150, his mouth set in a straight line. His ruddy complexion looked redder than usual against his gray beard, and I couldn't see his eyes through his black Ray-Bans. He said nothing.

I put my head down slightly, somehow time machining back to childhood, because the set of his mouth looked oddly like my mother's the day I accidentally stepped on my four-year-old neighbor's baby bunny.

We sped past small groves of trees surrounding my neighborhood, down a hill past the creek valley where I spent my childhood, then up Hospital Hill. I felt like we were traveling at ninety miles per hour, but I wasn't sure if that was due to the effects of the bourbon I had consumed that morning or not. My familiar neighborhood surroundings felt cold and solemn for the first time in my life.

As he flew down my street, I tentatively asked, "Do you know how this might end up?" Inwardly, I wondered if he could smell the alcohol on my breath, though I'd masked it with mouthwash in an expert, years-of-experience effort to remain undetectable.

Matt looked at me. I couldn't see his eyes through his sunglasses, but I imagined they carried a hint of sadness. Or maybe it's what I *wanted* to see: just a tiny ounce of compassion. I felt a glimmer of hope that he might view me as an individual who needed help, someone who desperately needed treatment.

"You were drinking in your office. At work. On a school day." It was a statement. His words sounded clipped but not mean, like he was announcing a football game (which he sometimes did on Friday nights). Like everything was happening so fast he couldn't get the words out quickly enough. His manner of speech was out of character for the convivial guy who normally slapped everyone on the back with a jolly, "How ya doin'?"

This was happening. I knew somehow this day would come. *I knew it*, though I wasn't prepared for it.

The realization slammed into me with the same force as when my drunk stepdad ran his car into the light pole at the Casey's gas station a mile from my house (I sat in the passenger seat, then, too, a fifteen-year-old, glass speckling my bloody forehead).

He pulled into the driveway of my tan house at the end of the cul-de-sac, the house with the lawn I had neglected last summer. My wife had nagged and nagged me to get outside, and I remember thinking there was no beer cup holder on the mower, so I relegated all mowing tasks to her.

Matt got out, walked around to the passenger side, and opened the door. He was so *quiet* as he watched me stumble out of the truck.

"Matt, I . . . I need help," I said pitifully, with a bit of a whine creeping into my voice, which I hated.

Matt sighed. He put his hand on my shoulder, the first kind thing he'd done since he escorted me out of my office. "I know. There'll be an investigation . . . "

He kept talking, but I stopped listening after he repeated "placed on administrative leave." In the back of my head, I wondered how to maneuver around the situation. I wondered how to get on to my next drink.

And yet, for the first time in all my drinking years, I heard a strong mental counter to the monster in my head. This time, another voice piped up, much fainter than the other, louder, more grating monster: *How am I going to survive this? Where do I go from here? My wife, my children, my community, my friends: What will they think?*

I trudged into the house after hitting the wrong garage door code several times. Matt watched from the driver's seat to ensure I made it inside.

I walked into the kitchen and tossed my coat on the table. I thought, "*Maybe an end to all of this might not be so bad. Maybe even an end to it all.*" It was about to be a very cold winter.

Chapter 2

The Fallout

> "And nobody is winning the war inside me."
>
> —Anonymous

There are moments in life where one may feel so detached from reality that he believes he might be dreaming (while not drunk). I've experienced this phenomenon daily over the last few years of sobriety, and I felt it intimately as I walked into my house that day. Dizzying is not a strong enough word.

After Matt backed down the driveway, I slowly walked into my beautiful home. The lit tree, Santas, poinsettias, candles, the smell of cinnamon and pine greeted me, as did the old ceramic Christmas tree that sits atop a lamp with little holes for clear plastic pegs—my daughter's favorite decoration. Despite the warmth surrounding me, my home was the last place I wanted to be. It's strange how home can seem so unwelcome during times of despair.

Sherman, our cockapoo, greeted me and instantly stopped wagging his tail. He felt my brokenness.

My God, what have I done?

I made my way into the living room and fell into my brown recliner. I heard a buzzing in my head, partly from the alcohol wearing off, partly from the shock of the situation.

My thoughts replayed what had happened over the last five hours, starting with my alarm.

At seven o'clock that morning, my eyes opened a crack, and I immediately thought, *God, my mouth's dry.* I'd drunk a fifth of . . . *something . . . vodka?* . . . while watching the Thursday night NFL game in bed and had conked out before halftime. I wondered if Alesha had covered me with our blue snowflake flannel sheets.

It took a minute to orient myself, to find the will to stand up, and to throw off the covers.

I did a brief mental inventory of the amount of vodka and energy drink I had left. *Damn!*

I was out of vodka *and* energy drink, fuzzily recalling that I *had* drunk vodka the night before. It looked like it'd be a Jim Beam and flat orange Crush kind of morning.

But first things first: I had to vomit in the sink (as I did most mornings).

As I heaved over the sink, I felt my abs work to move the process. Pain, like a scalpel digging into my skin, fired through my midsection. An incongruous thought came to mind: *Wow, I get a good ab workout every morning.*

I'd continue shaking and vomiting if I didn't drink alcohol almost immediately, so I poured roughly three shots of bourbon I'd hidden behind the toilet paper under the sink into the quarter liter of warm Crush I'd carelessly left uncapped on my bedside table the night before. Down the hatch went this disgusting concoction, burning my throat and making my eyes water. Almost immediately, I felt a jolt of nervous shock, and then . . . *euphoria*. The sweat, vomiting sensation, and anxiety fell away.

I had fed the Black Dog. I knew I'd be good for another couple of hours.

As I crouched over the sink, I avoided looking in the mirror, knowing I'd see a puffy-faced forty-four-year-old with bloodshot eyes sporting an unshaven face and greasy, graying hair.

Despite my refusal to look at myself, I still felt at peace, and above all else, satiated. After all, it was the Christmas season and all was well in my world—as long as I could get through a day of dealing with bathroom-vaping, class-skipping high schoolers.

I gargled cheap wintergreen mouthwash (by now, it made sense to buy the cheap stuff because I was using *a lot* of mouthwash). The cheap version stung less and tasted somehow staler than Listerine, but I thought it masked my vomit-and-bourbon breath. In my almost-constant drunken state, I figured I was good as new after a swig of the stuff.

I made my way upstairs where my wife, Alesha, and my kids, Boston and Tessi, and our niece who lives with us, Chelsey, were eating pancakes, checking their phones for the weather, and shouting, "Mom, where's my backpack?" I kissed Alesha (I inhaled deeply as I went in for the kiss in an effort to further disguise the scent of alcohol), said my good-byes to the kids, and grabbed my coffee. Sometimes I could stomach the French-pressed brew, sometimes I couldn't.

On the way to work, I stopped at a gas station for a Mike's Hard Lemonade, which I poured into an extra travel mug. It was all so casual, so practiced. Same gas station. Same attendant. Same Mike's Hard Lemonade, same routine every single day before work. If I didn't have it to take the edge off, the dreaded sweating would start, and my heart would begin to pound.

Once I arrived at school, I said hello to Sarah, our administrative assistant, and Marta, our school counselor (who people called my "work wife"), dropped off my laptop, and headed to the parking lot. It was my job to ensure my students (especially the ones with questionable driving skills) didn't do anything stupid. I shook hands, high-fived, and scolded where it was warranted. I tried to make kids feel welcome that Friday, whether they wanted to be there or not. Around 8:13, I knew the last of the procrastinators would sprint to the front doors of the high school, so I quickly ran to my car and took a swig out of the travel mug to keep the buzz going.

All better.

I made my way to my office and sorted through my emails before calling down the students I needed to meet about behavior and attendance issues. I had worn a vintage heather gray Lynx hoodie and jeans because our staff was allowed informal dress on Fridays, and I briefly thought how it might help the students see me as more human as I gently disciplined them.

I glanced at the clock after meeting with several students. *Almost lunch duty time.*

Like clockwork, I felt the itch of the Black Dog. It made me feel like I needed to scratch the middle part of my back but couldn't reach it. I could almost hear its goading, grating voice: *It's time, Pat,* it seemed to say.

I couldn't ignore it—I was powerless against it. I returned to the parking lot, opened my car door, and reached in to give my trusty travel mug a jiggle. I quickly judged I had about six or seven ounces left, a perfect amount to get me through the next few hours, maybe even the whole school day.

I tipped the travel mug back, and down it went.

Ahhhh . . . I closed my eyes briefly and slammed the driver's side door shut.

A movement to my right caught my eye as I registered my key card to open the door to the school. Matt, our school superintendent, walked toward me in long strides. He said in his characteristic greeting, "Hey Pat, do you have a minute?"

I smiled at him. "Sure! Do you want me to grab Hutch?" Hutch was the principal, a guy twenty years my senior, a proud Black man from the same streets I'd lived on for a few years: the east side of Des Moines. Whenever kids at school got in trouble, I knew they'd rather see me instead of Hutch, because he put up with exactly zero bullshit.

"No, let's go to your office," Matt replied. It wasn't unusual for Matt to stop in, though he usually asked for both Hutch and me, not me alone. As I sat at my desk and as Matt slowly shut the door, he took a seat in front of me, where students or parents usually sat. A feeling of foreboding flushed up my chest, not unlike sitting down in a too-warm hot tub (with a drink in hand, of course).

"I see you were at your car," Matt stated, and without preamble, asked, "have you been drinking?"

Holy shit, he didn't mince words.

I suddenly felt detached from my body, as if suspended near the yellowing ceiling tiles of my office, watching the scene from above our middle-aged heads. Was I dreaming? Did he *really* just say that?

His gray eyes bore into mine. He looked older at that moment, more weary. The lines in his forehead were deeper than I remembered, and a flush creeped up his neck like leaves making patterns on the trunk of a tree, all the way up his bald head. The flush had nothing to do with his usual golf-induced sunburn.

I had been yelled at by Marine Corps drill instructors who had killed men. I had been berated by football coaches in front of entire teams and community crowds, been verbally cut to the bone by past girlfriends (and Alesha, my wife, had screamed at me a fair amount, too), but all of that paled in comparison to the atomic blast I felt at those four simple words: *Have you been drinking?*

My heart felt like it was lunging at him from across the desk. *Oh shit! Think fast! How are you going to navigate this?*

There was no question. I had to lie.

"No," I replied, and suddenly, my throat constricted, as if my body was fighting against the gigantic untruth I'd just told.

"You haven't been drinking at all? If I searched your car, I wouldn't find any alcohol?"

"Uh . . . Just empties from last weekend." I leaned forward in my seat, desperate to communicate that the assorted collection of Mike's and Jim Beams riding around in the back of the car like wobbling pets were from previous days off school grounds.

He locked me in with his steely eyes. We looked exactly like a principal and a student who'd made a really bad decision (like drinking in the high school parking lot). "Pat, don't make me breathalyze you."

His gaze was so intense. I wondered briefly if he'd had some sort of training about tough conversations and that the training had suggested holding continual eye contact.

I looked away. I couldn't bear his gaze, and at that moment, I knew my turkey was cooked. Looking back, there were probably things I could've done to escape the ordeal, but at the moment my only thought was . . . *checkmate*.

I tried a different tactic anyway. "I'm in pain, Matt. My ankles hurt like hell all the time, and I've developed a drinking problem. I don't know what to do," I said, sounding so pitiful that I hated myself.

Silence dragged. I was amazed that the regular high school sounds of slamming lockers, the hum of conversation in the hallways—every so often punctuated by a holler from one of the rowdier kids in the school—disappeared. Or maybe it's because my ears were filled with the sound of my pounding heart.

"You know this reflects upon my license too, correct?"

"Yeah, I know . . . " My whole body tensed against my chair, my favorite, comfortable, worn office chair with the arms completely broken off. Inside, I suddenly felt terrified to leave it, and I'm sure my face communicated my panicked state. It was more than a chair. It was my entire livelihood. My way of putting my kids through college.

My heart tried to lob its way out of my chest again as Matt stood up. "Okay, you're on administrative leave. I need your keys and your computer, and take anything else you'll need in the immediate future."

I slowly handed him my school keys, complete with a free lanyard adorned with parading chicken nuggets that ironically stated, "Nugs, Not Drugs." I grabbed random books out of my office, all the while internally berating myself, *"What are you doing? What're the books for? For a beach vacation after you lose your job? Huh,* stupid?"

Matt continued to narrate his actions as if talking to a three-year-old. The thought occurred to me that he had to document every word he was saying—the school's lawyers were almost definitely involved. "Okay, I'm going to walk to my truck. In five minutes, you'll come out and I'll take you home."

He left. I stared at my degrees on the wall, unfinished discipline referrals on my desk, pictures of my family in frames. Like I was moving through Jell-O, I slowly stood up, the inexplicable stack of books still in my arms, and walked out of my office, not knowing if I was still Webster City High School's assistant principal.

Mercifully, nobody else in the office witnessed my walk of shame. They were all on lunch duty. I don't think I could have borne it if they were there. What would I say? *"Catch ya later?"*

My head throbbed. My buzz was starting to recede, and the Black Dog was stirring again. I clambered into the side of Matt's truck without saying a word. Every step felt as if I was marching toward the guillotine.

Later, I found out the teachers and administrators had set a trap for me. I wondered who'd been the "lookout," who'd been the "communicator," and who had said to Matt, "Go now! He's at his car! I can see he has that mug again . . ."

I imagined them as CIA operatives, talking into the cuffs of their sweatshirts on that dressed-down, warmish December day, all implicit in my demise. My friends, my colleagues, had betrayed me. The implications of these realizations would come crashing down later. At that point, all I could do was hang my head and hope nobody saw me leave the high school parking lot.

Back at home after the entire harrowing, dizzying, soul-crushing event, I stared at the wall for the next ninety minutes, Sherman sitting at my feet in confusion. It was about one o'clock in the afternoon. I imagined the goings-on back at school. Several of my chummier students, who I always made a point to speak with at lunch, were probably wondering where I was.

I pictured red-headed Jara, chewing on the end of her braid as usual, asking, "Where's Mr. Farley?"

Lexi would yell (she couldn't speak quietly, ever), flouncing down the hallway, "I saw him leaving with Mr . . . What's-His-Name? The superintendent?"

Well, this sucks, I thought. *Might as well grab a drink.*

No.

The Dog whispered, *You can't get through this ordeal without a drink.*

No!

My throat constricted.

Are you kidding? It's the worst day of your life, and look at you, starting to sweat again.

NO!

It was likely the first time I'd felt any amount of internal ferocity or monumental pushback toward the Black Dog.

I had to call someone. Principal Hutch, my good friend? He either knew and didn't want to get involved, or more likely, didn't know. I probably shouldn't have called, but I picked up my phone anyway.

"Hutch?" I said in a tentative voice.

"Pat! What the hell?" Hutch's booming voice flew through the phone and into my ear. "You mean to tell me you've been *drunk* every day? Are you freakin' kiddin' me, man?"

Tears fell. It was probably the first time in years I'd cried. Great, gulping heaves held all the sorrow, anguish, regret, and every ounce of fear I felt. I would be terminated or forced to resign, and how would I feed my family? How was I *here*, bewildered and still fucking drunk?

Oh, my God, my family.

I cried even harder.

"Pat? Pat?" Hutch said.

Something in his voice made me stop, and I mumbled, "Huh?"

"Listen to me, then I've gotta go. Are you thinking about hurting yourself?"

That was it? No assurances that everything would be all right? That if I submitted myself to a program, I'd be allowed to keep my job? Because—let's be honest—I knew on some level that I'd called him to feel some hope that I'd be allowed to come back.

"Absolutely, I'm thinking of hurting myself," I said, and with a flash of anger, hung up the phone. What was the point of talking to him if he wasn't going to help me keep my job?

My thoughts circled. *If I can't stop drinking, I'll continue to spiral and lose my wife and children. If I lose my wife and children, I won't want to live. If I don't want to live, I'll have to die. So am I supposed to generate some action plan as to how I might go about ending my life?*

But as always, my thoughts, like slippery eels, whipsawed and began to slither their way toward a new idea. *Maybe I can keep this from Alesha. Maybe she'd never have to know. You've read stories of guys going off to the bar or to the coffeehouse every day, pretending like they're at work. You can find a new job in ten days and then tell Alesha,* "Surprise! I found a new calling for my life and totally switched career paths!"

Yes, that could work, I thought in my still-muddled state. This wasn't that bad, something of a faux pas, really . . .

I don't have many friends that I could entrust with this, and there were only two or three people I thought I could reach out to who might help me with damage control. I decided to run this new idea by my good friend and neighbor, Todd, the school district food director. I figured that he would agree to keep my secret from Alesha, so I felt a huge sense of relief when he jackrabbited over as fast as he could, likely hearing the despondent tone in my voice. Sure enough, as soon as I saw him, I saw that worry had overtaken his thin, pale face, and he might have even been in the middle of preparing lunch because I saw BBQ sauce on his shirt.

Todd stared at the floor as I sobbed through my woe-is-me tirade, but his head popped up as soon as I finished.

"You need to call Alesha," he said flatly, seeing right through my portrayal as The One Who Had Been Wronged.

"No, I think I can find a way around . . ."

"Call her *now*," he interrupted.

Alesha, who is a nurse, was at a work Christmas party about an hour away. What a fabulous Christmas present I was bringing her: *"Hi, honey, I'm a loser who probably just lost his job and will likely be going through nervous alcohol withdrawal soon. Merry Christmas!"*

The phone call didn't go much differently than I'd imagined.

"Hi! What's up?" Alesha answered. I could hear people laughing in the background. Her colleagues. What would she tell *them*?

"I was sent home from work today for drinking," I said, skipping all the pleasantries. What was the point?

Silence. I could picture her face, her number eleven wrinkles above her nose practically crushing her forehead, just like so many other times I'd disappointed her. I'd noticed recently that her wrinkles didn't bounce away as quickly as they used to. When she finally spoke, she sounded rehearsed, as if she'd trained herself to say them when the time was right. I realized she probably had. She was a nurse, after all. She *knew*.

"Pat, you need help. You're going to the hospital tonight."

"No, no, I'm fine. I'll figure this out," I said in a hoarse voice, willing her to understand that I could smooth it all over. I was the head of the house, for God's sake. I was supposed to have a solution for everything.

You're going," Todd interjected in a firm voice, and I turned my back on him like little kids do when they think they're hiding.

"I'll be home in an hour or so, and then I'm taking you to the hospital," Alesha said abruptly, then hung up.

The kids came home, swinging their backpacks onto the hooks by our door and clamoring for snacks. If they thought it was weird that Todd and I were mutely sitting in the living room, they didn't show it. We tried for some faint laughter every now and then, but I began feeling a little shaky because it had been about four hours since my last drink.

After the kids disappeared to the basement, friends' houses, and their rooms, I said to Todd, "I wonder what my future with the school might look like?"

He paused. "I don't think they'll let you go." I don't know if he was trying to give me some false positive news or whether he really did believe it, but I didn't care. I felt a rush of relief anyway.

My relief was short-lived, because I heard Alesha's car pull in the driveway, and I was dreading our interaction. She looked furious when she saw me sitting with Todd, but I knew her well enough to know she'd never unleash on me in Todd's presence and within earshot of the kids. Her normally straightened blonde hair was pulled back into a ponytail, her hot pink scrubs were rumpled. Her green eyes shot icicles at the both of us. "Pack a bag. Let's go," she said between clenched teeth.

I protested. I don't even remember what I said, but it was something along the lines of, "I'll be fine," which of course, was ridiculous.

"No, Pat," she said. "We're going."
I sighed and went off to our room. I packed a small carry-on bag as if I'd be gone for just one night. In reality, I had no idea how long I'd be gone. Twelve pairs of underwear or two?

I settled for two.

Our fourteen-year-old son, Boston, watched me pack. "What's going on?" He looked more than a little nervous, his eyes darting between the bag I'd packed and my pale face. He probably thought his mom was kicking me out.

"*Shhh* . . . It's okay," I said, and suddenly, my memories rewound, screeching to a halt on a replay in my mind of something I'd witnessed as a child: my parents screaming at each other after a night of my stepdad's heavy drinking. I swore I'd never expose my children to it, and here I was, doing just that. For the second time in a day and the second time in years, I cried and pulled my son to my chest. I kissed his curly brown hair and walked out the door with my wife. I saw Todd awkwardly standing in the background, then watched as Todd pulled Boston toward him.

Of course he needed a hug, because his dad was such an *unbelievable fucking idiot*.

Alesha and I hardly spoke in the car. What was there to say? I felt nothing but shame, and as I stared out the window into the blackness, I saw millions of Christmas lights in the distance. They were so beautiful. I remembered how I'd loved gazing at Christmas lights as a child. I felt a bit like a child again at that moment, escorted by my angry wife to a definite unknown. Yes, yes, I was definitely still a child—an adult man would never have gotten himself into such a desperate situation.

We headed straight to Mary Greeley Hospital in Ames, and I realized that Alesha had either done her homework for when this day would come or had consulted her coworkers as soon as she found out I'd been led out of the high school. I didn't ask. Again, I felt like she was my mom and I was the misbehaving kid who had suddenly turned meek and submissive because I'd done something terrible and was headed off to juvenile detention.

"Here's what's going to happen. Once you get to the ER, you'll say you're having problems with alcohol and are about to experience some significant withdrawal symptoms," she said in the no-nonsense voice she uses with her patients, giving me a once-over and noticing my mild shaking and sweating.

The ER seemed busy, though I hadn't spent a lot of time in ERs and had no idea of their usual levels of activity. *Maybe they're so busy, they'll just send me home with some meds or something,* I thought.

I always thought detox or rehab would look like the pseudo-psychiatric environments in movies, a shoddy joint with terrible furniture and a black-and-white television chained to the wall. But the nurse took me to a normal exam room with cotton balls in jars on the counter. I promptly laid on a bed as she took my vitals and drew blood.

A middle-aged doctor with sandy hair conferred with Alesha. Knowing she was a nurse, he spoke with her as an equal. In between her sobs, he told her my blood pressure was 210/168, a "hypertensive emergency," and that I was severely potassium deficient. "I'm concerned about his kidneys. He could be suffering from acute kidney injury," the doctor said.

Acute kidney injury? Hypertensive emergency? Oh, shit.

Alesha's face immediately paled. She knew all the medical vernacular, and it was obvious that none of it was good.

They immediately set up an IV, began pumping potassium chloride, and gave me some other drugs to try to stabilize my blood pressure. Alesha could see my sides begin to heave, so she dove for the trash can and shoved it under my face just as I began vomiting. I was dizzy, shaking, sweating, and more miserable than I'd ever felt. As if I was experiencing every illness I'd ever had in my entire life, all at once.

Another doctor came in, visibly annoyed, a stethoscope around his neck. He looked like an old-time physician, with white hair and glasses that had slid down the length of his beaky nose. He barely looked me over before he said, "Nobody's coming to save you. You're addicted to alcohol and probably always will be."

Part of me thought, "Well, duh," and the other part of me wanted to punch his pointed nose flat. I closed my eyes, eased myself onto my back on the hospital bed, and for the millionth time that day, wondered how my life trajectory had landed me there. I wished the floor was quicksand, briefly remembering through a pounding head how I'd been obsessed with finding quicksand as a kid.

The doctors and nurses left, probably to confer about how they'd treat me. They said something to Alesha about using the CIWA-Ar scale to track my alcohol withdrawal syndrome severity to help them guide treatment, which I gathered had to do with all the questions they'd asked me when they admitted me (like, "Do you feel nervous?" and "Do you feel sick to your stomach?"). The room got quiet except for the beeping machines tracking my threatening vital signs.

Most individuals with alcohol use disorder experience mild alcohol withdrawal syndrome (AWS) symptoms: anxiety, headaches, nausea, vomiting, insomnia, and tremors. These symptoms, including mild autonomic hyperactivity (increased heart rate, blood pressure, and body temperature), usually begin within six hours after the last drink and last twenty-four to forty-eight hours. I was right there in that category.

A smaller group experiences severe complications, such as hallucination, seizures, or delirium tremens (DTs), which the doctors gauged when I arrived. Hallucinations typically appear between eight and twelve hours after the last drink, while seizures often occur within twelve to twenty-four hours. DTs, a life-threatening form of alcohol withdrawal, emerge within one to three days, causing confusion, altered consciousness, severe autonomic instability, and without treatment, sometimes death.

Alesha was sitting in the ugly orange plastic chair next to me. She began crying a new batch of tears.

"Are you going to leave me?" I asked through watery eyes. The thought of watching her packing up her shoes and clothes, kids in tow, caused me to begin retching again.

Why *wouldn't* the answer be yes? *Who in their right mind would stay?*

"No," she replied, "But this can't happen again."

I held my head over the trash can, and from what sounded like a mile away, the beaked stethoscope doctor said to Alesha, "Staying in the hospital to detox for the next few days . . . prescribing benzodiazepines to treat withdrawal . . . continuing potassium . . . blah, blah, blah . . ."

Benzodiazepines are the primary treatment for AWS because they mimic alcohol's effects in the brain, preventing withdrawal symptoms. They gave me the long-acting drug, Librium (the generic drug chlordiazepoxide), to reduce the risk of symptom recurrence. The doctors told Alesha they would gradually reduce the amount as my symptoms improved, and AWS would resolve within a week if I didn't consume alcohol.

With the word "benzos" ringing in my ears, I crouched over the trash can again. But for the first time in my life, I felt a *want*. This new *want* hit me like a tsunami. From that moment on, I knew I'd do everything I could to live sober. I'd do *anything* to kill the Cujo that puppeteered my brain for most of my life.

"I'm done," I said faintly.

Alesha rolled her eyes and started crying again. She'd heard it before.

I sat up, clutching at my eyes as tears squeezed between my fingers. "No, Alesha. Really! I'M DONE WITH THIS!"

Ironically, the Black Dog reverberated in my head immediately: *"You can't do this without me."*

Like a physical manifestation to a visceral response, my heart felt on the verge of exploding. My tremors got worse. If I'd been holding a glass of water, the water would have sprayed all over the floor, I was shaking so much. My temples felt as if I'd been headbutting a glass table. But I'd finally voiced the communique, the declaration: *I was going to kill the Black Dog, and I'd finally committed to the fight.*

It was getting late, so after they finally took me to my room by wheelchair, I encouraged Alesha to go home. Before she left, I hugged her like someone drowning, not unlike when my daughter was two and attached herself to my leg before I left for work every morning.

My eyes were heavy as barbells, but the nurses warned me they'd need to check me every three hours to monitor my condition. I reasoned that maybe even a fitful sleep would help me numb the worst day of my life.

Chapter 3

Shame

"The loneliest moment in someone's life is when they are watching their whole world fall apart, and all they can do is stare blankly."

—F. Scott Fitzgerald, *The Great Gatsby*

If you pop onto any social media site, it doesn't take long to find a video of a teacher in an office, door closed, being interrogated by the principal and/or a police officer about being under the influence while teaching.

Drunk! At school, while working with kids? What kind of person does that?

Me. I am that person.

I called it the Black Dog.

But the Winston Churchill-inspired name seems incompatible with my pleasurable, seductive, loving friend in a bottle. For decades, it provided near-instant euphoria to all of my senses. It brought laughter to weekends, social bonding to holidays, popularity, social rewards at sports outings, an identity, a companion to all things fun! My relationship with alcohol was *so* dear to me.

The French philosopher Blaise Pascal said, "We are only truly happy when dreaming about future happiness." I understand that sentiment intimately; the prospect of the next long-awaited drink always put a smile on my face. The pleasure of anticipation and each first sip offered endless bounds of happiness. The feeling that alcohol brought and the social "coolness" that accompanied it was an easy tradeoff for the hangovers, paunchy body, and jab to my wallet. I liked who I was with alcohol, but it had so much more in store for me than just fun.

In the hospital, I recall waking throughout the night nurse shift changes, sweating and shaking, seeing grotesque things like terrifying pinscher demons with gnashing teeth and fiery tongues. I was so confused, drifting in and out of sleep and in a dreamlike state I'd awaken shaking and unable to grasp where I was.

There really are no words to describe the despair that began to set in as the morning came. It's one thing to be depressed about letting down everyone you know and everyone you've ever cared about. But this level of depression alongside alcohol withdrawal is its own special kind of hell.

What had happened to my seductive lover? How had it dumped me in a hospital bed?

Here's what it came down to: I thought I could handle the drinking on my own, even as the urges perpetually became stronger and stronger with time. I fought them, keeping sacred the alcohol-free hours of leaving for work in the morning until arriving home in the evening.

But the enemy penetrated those gates. Physical withdrawal was somewhere between having to sneeze (and not quite being able to) and waiting as long as possible to go to the bathroom after a long car ride. To combat it, I'd shift, take off my seatbelt—as if somehow different actions would help—but the physical urge didn't dissipate. Mentally, the addiction penetrated my rational mind, and one day, it convinced me to take a drink before work. Just one tiny drink to kill the hangover.

Stop quick and grab a drink at the convenience store. Nobody will know.

Somehow, "I" became a "we," as if the Black Dog and I were a duplicate personality: We're *better at our job with a drink!* We're *funnier,* we're *more energetic with a drink.*

And so it happened: eight-hour gaps between drinks became five-hour gaps, which became three-hour gaps . . . which led to no gaps.

Somehow, I came to believe that if I kept my stash in my car, it wouldn't be that big of a deal: *"Think of the movie* Charlie Wilson's War. *He drank all day, people loved him, and he practically ended the Cold War!* Mad Men: *They drank all day! We're no different, Pat. There's no shame in this."*

And so, one day I decided I should drink periodically throughout the school day. I was more patient with the kids, more understanding with the teachers, better able to engage and participate in meetings. *That's been the issue the whole time*, I concluded. *If I can just have access to alcohol throughout the day, I'm better!*

I made it until the end of the 2022-2023 school year, and until July, when I was off contract for a month. I swore that once I returned in August for the 2023-2024 school year, this Black Dog nonsense would stop. I thought, *I'll even take ten days off from drinking before the school year starts. That will get me in shape to roll back the clock with this alcohol stuff so I can have a great school year.*

My vow lasted one day and nine hours.

One weekend in October 2024, I was working on a few loose shingles on my roof. Wasps living in a nest hidden in my roof began swarming me, and I fell off the ladder, breaking both ankles. If ever I needed an excuse to drink heavily, it was compound fractures in both ankles. Before long, I decided that it was time for a drink whenever I wanted. My ankles hurt like hell.

Back in the hospital, a different Black Dog—the kind that had signaled Churchill's depression—slinked into my life. *What have I done? What have I become?*

The nurses who checked my vitals and medicine levels were kind and caring, but all I could think about was getting back to my normal life.

I tried to watch TV, but my mind was in a holding pattern: *Do I still have a job? A life?* I still had my wife and kids, but what were they doing without me? What were they telling people? I spent a lot of time trying to predict what Matt and the school board might do with me.

Visitors began trickling in. I was amazed by the fact that people took time out of their schedules to visit me in the hospital, but at the same time, I felt unending shame. I didn't deserve these people's sympathy. Hospital visits were for people with cancer, not people who guzzle vodka for fun!

Unbelievably, Hutch, the principal, was my first visitor. He propped up some chocolates on my side table and awkwardly patted me on the shoulder. I wanted to curl under the covers and disappear. Before this travesty, I was set to become the next principal upon his retirement, and we had discussed this eventuality from time to time while socializing.

He stayed twenty minutes or so, centering the conversation around my health: How was I feeling? Was I getting around okay? Was I bored? I noticed that despite our friendship, he carefully danced away from any job-related questions, like, "I bet you can't wait to get back to work!"

I surmised that my ascent to the head high school principal position was now highly unlikely. When he left, I jammed my palms into my eyes, filled with a fresh bout of regret and despair.

Later that morning, my sister, Sherie, brought pictures of us and some other small gifts. My brother-in-law, Hank, and my good friends, Erik and Audel, visited as well. Though it was so nice of them to show they cared about me, I hated the reason they were there. I despised being the "weak link on the team" and hated having people worry about me.

What had I done?

It was addiction's other tactic. It whispers seductively, *All you need is a drink. Others don't understand you like I do. I'm your refuge, your one true love.*

Aside from dealing with family members and friends awkwardly asking, "Pat, you sure you're okay?" and continually craving alcohol, I also discovered I couldn't breathe very well. Apparently, my lungs weren't used to breathing sober air. They felt like two mammoth sponges weighing down my chest. I wondered if it was how heavily pregnant women feel.

The shaking, vomiting, and sweating had slowly let up due to the Librium pumping into my veins, but Alesha, who had come to visit later in the day, was solution-oriented, chatting with the doctors, discussing further evaluation after detox and a treatment plan. She was cordial and caring toward me, though I wondered if I would have acted the same way if our roles had been reversed. I doubted it—if I had been left to my own devices to negotiate homework and bedtimes, burn chicken nuggets for dinner, and lift dog crap out of the yard alone, I may have been a real bear.

Because I was thinking of her and everything she had going on at home, I was reluctant to agree to inpatient treatment and wanted to manage my alcohol problem as an outpatient.

She was having none of it. We argued a bit, but it ended with her saying flatly, "You've got to do inpatient."

"I guess that's that," a nurse, one of the cheekier ones with frizzy red hair, said from the corner of the room, where she was checking the tubing for my medicine, so I shut up and accepted it, vowing to start the argument again the next morning.

Alesha left in the late afternoon of that first day in the hospital, after the doctor came in and stated that he did not like what he saw in my bloodwork. My friend Erik stayed with me that night, before I received a heavier Librium dosage. That and other drugs lulled me to sleep. My last memory that night was of Erik getting me a blanket and tucking me in. Erik was one of the hardest, unsympathetic people I knew, and if he was tucking me in, I knew I was in deep shit.

Sure enough, that night, I had a recurring nightmare about losing my job, and when I awoke in the morning, all I wanted was a drink.

Alesha returned in the morning and insisted we weren't leaving without a substance abuse evaluation and a referral, so a social worker arrived that afternoon. He was a jovial guy in his late fifties or early sixties with short, salt-and-pepper hair and round glasses.

I'd been through substance abuse evaluations before with my regular doctor (who I'm sure strongly suspected I was an alcoholic) but I was always evasive or didn't fully answer her questions. This time, I decided to be honest with the social worker, particularly because Alesha was sitting right there and would see through any bullshit answers.

"Okay, Pat. Here we go. Do you ever feel cravings or urges to drink alcohol?" The social worker asked in a way-too-energetic voice, as if he was thrilled he'd finally gotten an "interesting" case—a mangled wreckage of a man with a life in tatters.

"Yes," I replied.

He made a little tapping sound on his computer, then looked over his glasses at me.

"Has your substance use affected your work or school performance?"

I snorted at that one. "Uh, yes."

"Do you continue to use substances even when they cause problems in your life?"

"Yes."

"Have you ever engaged in risky behaviors, like driving under the influence or having unsafe sex while under the influence?"

I glanced at Alesha, who was looking at the speckled white floor, and cleared my throat. "Yes, um, the first one."

"Have you noticed that you need to use more of a substance to get the same effect?"

"Yes."

"Has your drinking pattern changed over time, such as increased frequency, drinking alone, switching types of alcohol?"

"Yes."

"Do you ever drink in the morning or to steady your nerves?"

"Yes."

"Have you ever hidden alcohol or lied about your drinking to family, friends, or coworkers?"

"Yes."

"Have you had blackouts or memory loss due to drinking?"

"Yes," I mumbled.

"How often?"

"Every week?" I replied. "I dunno, it varies."

"Do you ever drink to the point of passing out?"

"Yes."

"How often does this happen?"

"Every night?" I replied, my voice rising as if I was the one asking the question.

I answered every question "yes," and Alesha looked more and more dumbfounded, which surprised me.

The social worker began talking to us with his head cocked, a signal I'd come to associate with hospital-related bad news. "You're at the highest possible risk for relapse. Inpatient treatment is the only type of treatment I'd recommend for you."

Alesha pressed her lips together. She'd won the argument.

About an hour later, a doctor came in for an evaluation and released me from the hospital, asserting that my vitals seemed somewhat stable. I felt a bit untethered. Had the hospital followed the right protocol? How could they drop this huge bombshell on me and then say, "You're a disaster waiting to happen, but oh, well, we've done all we can do. Go get 'em, champ!" (As I discovered later, the care and treatment for substance use disorders leaves a lot to be desired.)

I was ready to get home (and I hated to admit it, desperate for a drink). More than that, I couldn't wait to hug my kids—I didn't know what types of messages had been conveyed to them during my time in the hospital and I didn't ask—but I knew they knew it probably involved alcohol. No language spinning was going to cover that up; they weren't stupid.

When I finally got home and sank onto my couch, I mentally reviewed my time in the hospital. It marked the lowest point in my shattered life. I instinctively groped for a beer while sitting on the couch, as if it were just out of reach, shaking, always shaking.

When I take on new things, I usually give myself between an eighty to ninety percent chance of success, but with sobriety, I honestly gave myself a fifty-fifty chance of succeeding. But I also knew that failing at sobriety would mean the end of my marriage and family. Even so, I wasn't sure how much reinvention, renewal, and goal-oriented positivity I could muster.

To be frank, It all sounded terrible. The problem was that my "good" and my "normal" were anchored by alcoholism. I didn't know any other way to live, and in one way or another, alcohol had been the key source of my perceived happiness for twenty years or so. Over the last two or three years, it had total command. The Black Dog would not simply go quietly into the night.

I came home from the hospital on Tuesday, December 12, without the will to do much of anything at all. I was more exhausted than I'd ever been, was still experiencing withdrawals, and was *so* mentally, physically, and spiritually defeated. My entire stream of consciousness was a ship-sized wreckage of confusion and pain.

I was dreading one task: talking about this situation with the kids. When I walked through the door, I hugged my kids as I have never hugged them before. Alesha and I sat the kids down by the fireplace. I explained that too much beer had been hurting my stomach, and that I would not drink alcohol ever again.

Tessi, age thirteen, brightened. She said, "This'll be the best Christmas ever!"

Fourteen-year-old Boston was stone-faced. Both kids had spent hours in my work office before and after school. Prior to that, they often visited me in my high school classroom and college lecture halls. Both had high hopes of experiencing high school with me in their building someday, especially Boston. Although my becoming a principal had lost its luster to him, it pained me to know I'd potentially killed the opportunity just as my kids were coming up in the high school ranks.

During that first day, Alesha and the kids were sometimes around, sometimes not. Alesha made arrangements for friends to swing by and check up on me and take me to lunch. I think she was concerned I might hurt myself, and like it or not, the thought was often lurking in the back of my mind.

Every drop of alcohol had been removed from the house with the aid of our friends and neighbors, Todd and Lori, and their sons, Jordan and Carson. My basement bar looked ghostlike, and its featured beer signs, flags, neon lights, and random souvenirs looked forlorn and dusty, a blatant reminder of evaporated good times.

A week after I came home, I ended up in my doctor's office. For two years, my doctor, Angela Oelrich, had been concerned about my increased blood pressure and rising liver enzymes. She asked me about my drinking habits, and I responded with the usual lie: "Occasionally I party hard, but not often."

She advised me to cut back on the booze, exercise, and clean up my diet because my liver was growing fatty.

I finally had to face her after the all-too-public fallout and find out how bad things had gotten. My results from the hospital's blood tests were in. The familiar hospital smell assaulted my nostrils as Alesha and I checked in, and my mood immediately plummeted. The smell made me feel empty and depressed. I grabbed a *People* magazine, and instead of reading it, looked over it at each person in the waiting room.

Did that nurse know about me? The receptionist? Were they talking about me?

I was sure everyone knew about my downfall, and that led to a self-centered paranoia I couldn't shake. It didn't help that we lived in a small town, where everyone knew everyone. I imagined the rumors: *Did you hear about Pat Farley, the assistant principal? Yeah, drinking at work, with kids in and out of his office. What kind of idiot does that?* . . .

My thoughts idled, and I vividly remember thinking about how I've come to believe that people—across nearly every setting—can be grouped into thirds. Again and again, the pattern has held true in my life: One third of the people I've interacted with genuinely like me. One third can take me or leave me. And one third simply didn't care for me, whether quietly or with visible disdain.

It showed up in my classrooms. One third of my teachers were absolute rock stars—inspiring, wise, unforgettable. Another third were average, still finding their footing. And the final third: novice, disengaged, or simply not suited for the work.

This dynamic applied to my public reception within the community after they found out about my transgressions. Some showed real concern by treating me with respect. Others remained neutral, unbothered by my presence. And some eyes that once lit up in my presence now avoided mine entirely;

they looked past me, or worse, glared at me with contempt. (*"Shhhh . . . It's the alcoholic principal."*)

I don't say this with bitterness, just recognition. The balance of admiration, indifference, and resistance is part of the human experience. And knowing where I stand has helped me focus on those who truly matter—the ones who still show up. When people least deserve compassion and caring, they often need you the most.

I understood just how many people truly cared about me (and how badly I was hurting them) but it was uplifting to see friends stop by, including Tyler. Tyler and I have been good friends since high school, and like most friendships, we'd had our ups and downs. One morning in the thick of it all, Tyler rang the doorbell.

"Let's talk," he said. I could see myself reflected in his sunglasses, looking depressed beyond words, but I invited him in anyway. We went back to my sunroom and closed the door. I unloaded and broke into tears. He wanted to listen and offer whatever help he could, financial or otherwise. (Later, when I began treatment, Tyler offered to ride with me to the sessions.) Another companion who has been by my side, Laura, stopped over as well. We had become good friends during my time at the school. A history nerd like me, we discussed all things history, politics, etc. In recovery, you really do find out who your friends are.

"Hi, Pat," a familiar voice greeted us. My thoughts zoomed back to the present—the dreaded appointment. The voice belonged to Heather, a friend of ours who was also Dr. Olerich's nurse. Her husband, Eric, had taken me out to lunch a few days ago to ensure I didn't "off" myself.

She led me to the scale.

"Oh, you're down ten pounds," she said pleasantly.

It's easy when you don't eat, I thought.

My blood pressure was 138/85, which was a miracle considering what it had been in the hospital. Dr. Olerich bustled into the room in her usual style, quickly with her long red hair pulled back. Her dark eyes peered at me apprehensively through her thick-rimmed glasses. I half-expected a long lecture about the dangers of lying to your doctor for years, but Dr. O. didn't waste time in presenting the bad news.

"Your bloodwork is extremely concerning, especially your liver enzymes. I'm not sure I've ever seen liver enzymes this high in anyone your age," she paused, possibly to gauge whether I was ready to take the news seriously or not. "They will continue to increase for another week or two. If they don't decrease after six weeks, chances are, the damage is permanent and cirrhosis will have taken your liver."

I hung my head and stared at the ground. We discussed the mind-numbing "eventualities"—death or a waitlist for a liver transplant—and left it at that. Dr. O prescribed a host of medications for me, including an anti-anxiety medication. I was against these and anti-depressants, because I was fearful of the side effects, but to give me a realistic chance at beating this thing, I was willing to give them a try. Looking back, I'm glad I did.

I asked Alesha to step out of the exam room for a minute.

After she shut the door behind her, I looked into Dr. O's big brown eyes and said, "I misled you about my drinking, which prevented you from treating me, and I'm sorry."

She stared into my eyes. "Don't beat yourself up, Pat."

I had always been under the impression that alcoholism had impacted Dr. O's life in some terrible way. The tears in her eyes as she left the exam room told me that my situation had stirred up alcohol-related pain she also carried, and tears dripped down her cheeks as she left the exam room and as she walked past Alesha, who was sitting right outside the room.

Yet another caring person I indirectly hurt because I embraced my glorious love affair with alcohol.

What now? What next? After my
appointment with Dr. O., this was the rhythm
of my thoughts in this purgatorial existence I
brought myself: *What now? What next? What
now? What next?*

Eventually, I decided to see what I could do
with the carnage of my once-successful career.
I worked up the courage to look up my teacher
and principal credentials online through the
Iowa Board of Educational Examiners.

Everything seemed intact.

*Hmm . . . They haven't filed on my license
yet, so they probably won't,* I thought.

I called Jason at Woodward Academy. Both
of us were Marines, and he and I had run the
highly structured floor of Woodward Academy
for two years. We were like brothers, and I was
in desperate need of favors from friends. After
explaining my situation to him, Jason assured
me that the Academy would take me back with
open arms and that all would be well. The pay
would obviously be different, but at least I
would have a job, which gave me great relief.

Finally, I felt a glimmer of hope that I
might survive. I also felt a strange sense of
relief that I could avoid returning to a job I
loathed—in some ways, I was glad I'd found
the off-ramp, even if it wasn't the way anyone
with an above-seventy IQ would go about it.
The upshot of it all was that I knew I would
find a way to make more money.

About a week after leaving the hospital, I slowly walked down the stairs to the bar in my basement. Beer signs, flags, random souvenirs representing past drinking adventures, and small neon lights greeted me. The alcohol which gave life to the jubilant atmosphere had been removed, excommunicated.

A small thought occurred to me: *I bet they missed one bottle.*

I walked around to the server side of the bar and reached to the very back of the shelf. I drew out a cherry oak wine box secured with a silver-plated lock. I slowly opened it, half-hoping it would be there, half-hoping it wouldn't.

It was there. A bottle of single malt. I picked it up, hands still shaking, very much fighting withdrawal. As I touched it, it seemed as though my body instantly detected its presence: "It's here! It's here!"

I was amazed at its lightness, its lovely green color. I swear it gleamed, like in cartoons where the bad guy picks up the forbidden sword or the illicit jewel. The numen pale brown whiskey inside contrasted the emerald bottle. *Such complex sophistication.*

I set the bottle on the bar and rested my head in my hand a couple of inches from it, and I talked to it. "I thought we had a deal. Why did you turn on me? You took almost everything from me."

I began to cry. I wanted so badly to surrender, to drink from this enemy who didn't care, didn't agree, didn't disagree, didn't hate me, didn't do anything except possess the key to my real happiness.

How could I resist its seductive tug for the rest of my days?

Remarkably, I put the bottle back in the box.

But why? To save for *later*?

Chapter 4

It's Always Darkest Before it's Black

"The horror! The horror!"

— Kurtz, *Heart of Darkness*

Not knowing was my canary in a coal mine. I noticed my district email had been shut down on the way home from the hospital—not a good sign. My defense mechanisms were hard at work and bouncing around in my head: *Relax, Pat. The school district's lawyers temporarily shut it down.*

I tried to stay busy around the house, even painted a permanent smile on my face for the kids, but I was struggling in every way one could. Basic tasks seemed impossible: brushing my teeth, eating, putting on socks—all felt like they required heart surgeon-level concentration. I had called Matt twice in an effort to update him, but he'd had yet to answer. I'd been around education long enough to know an investigation was underway, and lawyers had counseled Matt not to speak with me.

I slept ten to twelve hours a day.

On Friday, December 15, Matt finally returned my call. "Hey Pat, can you come to the office so we can talk?"

I tried not to sound like a teenager getting a promposal as I squeaked, "Yes! *Yes!* Right now? I'll be right there!"

I felt a glimmer of hope.

Maybe I'm too valuable for him to let go. After all, I have a disease. He wouldn't fire someone who had heart disease or cancer, would he?

Of course not.

Alesha and our neighbors, Todd and Lori, who were hanging out in our living room, perked up when they heard the call. I flew into a frenzy. I couldn't get out the door to see Matt soon enough. I had showered but my curly hair wasn't gelled (it looks ridiculous without product), but nonetheless, I threw on slacks and a dress shirt and dashed to my car.

Alesha called after me, "Honey, maybe you should dress nicer!"

I barely listened; I was locked in on seeing Matt. As I drove, I felt as if I was watching myself in a movie as I pulled into the administration building parking lot like I had done so many times. I had worked so hard to ascend to secondary administration and land my dream job. Would the ride continue?

I remember walking toward the door, once again feeling like I was watching myself on a screen. I wasn't dressed exceptionally well, but

I had worn nice dress shoes. Ridiculously, I thought, "Matt will like my shoes. Maybe he'll keep me if he sees these shoes.

I opened the glass door and walked through another set of double doors. The Webster City Community School District building used to be a bank, and it still smells sterile, like old money and fat cat offices. I had always liked entering this building. It made me feel important. Historic pictures and framed pieces of the district's history adorned the walls. I loved this district. It was my home, my wife's home, my kids' home, though I had come to loathe the job.

A thought entered my head on my way in, one that will haunt me forever: *Do I hate this job? Or do I hate the fact that it interfered with my drinking? If I were sober, would I effectively be able to perform this important work?* Like many "what ifs" that one wrestles with in recovery, I'll never know.

Mary-Ellen, the head secretary, with whom I had a great working relationship, stood up behind her desk as soon as I walked in. She burst into tears, slowly walked toward me, and enveloped me in a giant hug.

My first thought: *Oh good! A homecoming! She's treating me like a heart attack victim!* My second thought: *This is actually* not *good at all . . .*

Matt's office was right around the corner from Mary Ellen's desk. I slowly made my way to the door and let myself in. He stood up from his desk, reached across it, and shook my hand. "It's good to see you, Pat," he said. He might as well have been wearing sunglasses, because I couldn't read his expression. But the way he moved toward me and gripped my hand felt like the old days. I felt a surge of hope.

He sat back down behind his desk. I sat on a black molded plastic chair across from him. *The principal versus the student.*

Without preamble, he said, "Pat, I'm going to need you to resign."

I heard a buzzing in my ears, and my face instantaneously warmed.

Shakily, I blew out a breath. "Is there anything I can do to move you from that?" I was faintly conscious that I'd used a weird choice of words.

"Look, an OWI . . . maybe. But . . . you were . . . " Despite his inability to hold a thought together, his steely eyes poured into mine. They looked faintly surprised.

"I know."

"If you resign, you'll be able to control the narrative some."

I nodded, and the buzzing grew louder. I vaguely heard him say he'd pay me out through the new year, that I could keep my benefits until then. He needed a letter of resignation. The word reverberated throughout the room

like a church ceiling: *resignation—nation*
—ation.

For about the millionth time in the past week, I was dumbstruck. I had no real behaviors or mindsets that allowed me to process, let alone cope. This was the cherry on top.

How would I go on? What kind of life would I have left? How was I going to pay bills, fight the urges to drink, and insulate my family from all of this?

I mumbled something to my former boss—*former boss! God, how had I gotten here?*—and stumbled out of his office. Mary-Ellen was still crying as I made my way past the beautiful Webster City office, an office I was no longer a part of.

Driving home, I felt as if I was in slow motion, and I'd be lying if I said I wasn't tempted to pull into Casey's. It would be so easy to pull into the gas station, to tip a bottle onto the counter and pay with cash. *After a frantic uncapping of the bourbon, it'd be so easy to let blessed relief slide down my parched throat. So easy.* I could almost taste the whiskey, that old familiar burn whispering promises of numbness and escape.

Instead, I gritted my teeth and drove home.

Why'd I stay out of the Casey's?

Here's why: Matt's resignation request punched me square in the chest. It was sharp, disorienting, and personal. I saw my wife's face, the quiet strength she carries. I thought of my kids—their laughter, their trust, their need for me to stay steady. I felt the damage I was experiencing, not just professionally, but almost spiritually, at the heart of my very being. The mental pain was real, raw, and loud. This was utter ruin, and what was worse, I was bringing dishonor to everyone I knew.

Todd and Lori were still sitting on the living room couch when I returned, as if I'd pushed pause on a giant remote before I left to hear Matt's edict. Lori searched my eyes and must have guessed the truth, because she quickly whispered, "Alesha's upstairs in the bedroom." I saw her whip her head toward Todd—ready, I assume, to speculate about what had happened.

Whatever. Who cared? My life was over anyway.

Step by slow step, I went upstairs and entered our bedroom. Alesha, who had been lying on the bed, quickly sat up. Her hair was sticking up all over like a porcupine, and it dawned on me for the thousandth time how much stress my actions were putting on her. I dreaded what I had to tell her next.

"What did he say?" Her eyes were round, beseeching. Willing the news to be good.

"I have to resign." I couldn't meet her eyes.

She slowly collapsed to our bed, buried her head in a pillow, her shoulders heaving as violently as if someone was shaking her. I stood there, both motionless and emotionless. I simply could not process the pain and suffering, and of course, I was craving alcohol like a shark craves blood. My left hand began shaking.

Numbly, I simply walked away, running my hand against the oak banister, feeling a part of my home that I'd no longer be able to afford. Downstairs, Todd was waiting. His hands were in his pocket.

He tried to cheer me up, but I ignored him. A voice in my head took the mic. *We may not survive this, Pat. It's time to draft options here: a plan A, B, and ultimately C, which is likely where all of this will go.* I shivered at the voice's cryptic meaning.

I was truly lost, mentally and emotionally. I think I experienced another rock bottom once I had to resign, after the initial tortuous stages of withdrawal. I faced an unrecognizable reality, fraught with consequences, fear, and despair—truly a hell of my own making.

After staring off into nothingness for hours, Alesha came downstairs, her eyes puffy and bright green. We sat at the kitchen table, apart yet together. Our hands alternately touched, then bounded away from each other, and we tried to focus long enough to formulate a game plan. We agreed treatment for me was our number one priority. It was obvious from my appearance alone that despite my best mental intentions, the drink was still very much the enemy at the gate.

Later that night, I got a call from Alesha's brother, Hank. Hank said an old college friend of his who worked as a reporter at KCCI, our local Des Moines-based news station, had called him about a soon-to-air story regarding a high school assistant principal and his untimely resignation.

"I beg you not to air this," Hank said to his friend. Hank, who is an accountant and successful business owner, sounded choked up on the phone. Careers and money are extremely important to Alesha's family, and I'm sure this development in our family tree was devastating. I left the conversation unclear as to whether the story would air or not.

I went upstairs and found Alesha fixing a casserole. She was staring at it intently, as if she were distracting herself. The small television we kept in the kitchen was on, and a lightbulb managed to go off in my ravaged brain.

She already knew the story would air.

Sure enough, as I turned from the fridge, KCCI's familiar trumpeting music fired up. I noticed the kids weren't around. I wondered if she'd sent them to friends' houses, just in case.

"Webster City High School is now looking for a new assistant principal," Laura Terrell, the familiar blonde anchor on weekdays at five, said in her clear, Midwestern accent. "The board unanimously accepted Patrick Farley's resignation this morning, and it's effective immediately."

The screen faded from Laura's face to my own face in a little blue box. They'd gotten ahold of my latest school portrait. A bulleted list appeared on the TV screen:

- Resignation accepted unanimously
- Special meeting Monday
- Effective immediately

"KCCI has not been able to confirm what led to the resignation. When asked, the district says, 'Because this is a personnel matter, we cannot share further details at this time.' The district says it has begun the process to look for Farley's replacement and says it is focused on meeting the needs of students and employees for the rest of the school year," Terrell continued.

KCCI must have been unable to secure a confirmed credible source that my resignation was alcohol related, so I thought, "No big deal! Slow day in the news!" (Defense mechanisms are so soothing.)

But the truth was, my embarrassment had spread, rapid-fire, beyond immediate colleagues, friends, and family. The larger community knew the truth about the tragedy of Patrick Farley, the disaster that he was. Any semblance of a legacy that I may have built was shattered. Any esteem I was held in, permanently tarnished. And my enemies must have only felt delight.

As my anger and anxiety began to rise, my left hand shook again, and the Black Dog whispered, *Now is the time to come back to me. It's on TV now. They don't want you anymore. Nobody loves you as I do.*

I shoved my left hand into my pocket and grabbed a Sprite out of the fridge. Alesha slammed the casserole into the oven and went upstairs to our room. The kids returned and we ate without her. I was too emotionally exhausted to reassure her, and when I went up to bed, she was asleep, her hair matted with tears.

It's easy to say, "so-and-so's life is ruined," but it's quite another to actually experience your own life ripped to shreds at your feet. I'd worked hard and had beat odds to get where I was in life, all to ruin it all by myself. I was usually capable of rebounding from setbacks and challenges, but didn't know whether I was capable of persevering. Conquering my drinking and rebuilding my career seemed insurmountable. I didn't even know where to start, and then adding a giant dollop of shame and self-hatred on top of all that—it was enough to push even the strongest person down.

Yet I had told my students and players a million times: "Get up, dust yourself off, create a vision, find courage, be brave, and never give up." It was the Marine in me that gave me hope at rejuvenation, though realistically it seemed quite impossible, what with depression setting in hard, zero appetite, and lots of sitting, sleeping, and staring off into space.

Things continued to devolve. Shortly after my fifteen minutes of fame on KCCI, I received certified mail from the Iowa Board of Educational Examiners announcing they were investigating me for ethical violations and to have my administrative and teaching licenses revoked. The reality hit me: *I may never teach again.*

Our savings dwindling, I had no real prospects. All my calls to connections fell on deaf ears, and a return to Woodward Academy probably wouldn't happen due to my educational license revocation.

A few days after my big KCCI debut, I contacted a few of the inpatient and outpatient facilities to weigh our options from the contact information we received from the substance abuse social worker in the hospital. I wasn't opposed to a thirty-day inpatient program, and I had about two months left on my health insurance through the school district. It became clear to Alesha and me that there were virtually no state-run options because whoever was in charge deemed my addiction not "severe" enough because I had no criminal incidences.

So it came down to the for-profit organizations that may or may not accept your insurance *after* you put down up to $30,000. *Um . . . out of the question.*

It quickly became clear why addiction recovery rates are so low. When those of us living with addiction look for help, our options are extremely limited unless we're an outright menace to society or have a ton of money. The rest of us live in the gray area of "figure it out on your own."

Ultimately, we decided I'd start with an intensive inpatient option. The program called for group meetings three times per week for three-hour sessions. It felt good to have a plan; it secured my footing to leave the Black Dog behind. I constantly reflected on the words I'd said aloud to Alesha: *"I'm done with THIS!"*

I've taken on many challenges in my life: I became a Marine, I won (or tried to win) football games, coached previously winless teams to the playoffs, got a degree, raised my children right, and tried to be a good husband, father, son, and friend. It was me versus whatever challenge lay ahead. I had full access to all of my faculties to put forth every ounce of effort and ability I possessed. With alcoholism, the game changed. The hardware I had to succeed had been hijacked. In the early stages of sobriety, you have some access to this hardware, but not much. In these early stages of sobriety, my mind was a battleground inside my head. The good guys were vastly outnumbered. I constantly felt a storm of emotions: sorrow, anger, mania, sometimes simultaneously.

Seventeen days after Matt brought me home, Christmas arrived. Christmas is generally a difficult time for some people, but prior to that year, not for me. Every Christmas morning, I'd roll across my pillow with a huge grin on my face. During childhood Christmases, my Dad would set aside any business stress and anger (which he would often displace on his kids) and put on a happy face. My mother would light up, bustling around the kitchen, giving us three helpings of everything. The happy day always covered up the usual pain of daily life our family experienced, and I had always tried replicating that joyful experience for my family.

That Christmas, the second my head rolled across the pillow, the blackness that saturated every crevice of my brain threatened to destroy any possibility of making happy memories.

Count your blessings, Pat. You still have your family. I put on a happy face and did my best to stave off my worries for the day; I knew they'd be waiting for me later.

Alesha, the kids, and I had our typical family morning Christmas. Late in the morning, we headed to Alesha's family's Christmas get-together in Ames. Alesha's parents, John and Rachel, always put on a jovial Christmas celebration with presents and a holiday feast. I was expecting the worst, thinking they'd either give me the cold shoulder or potentially even unload about my recklessness.

On the contrary, they could not have been more affectionate. They showered me with hugs. Alesha's sister, Amy, had already briefed her husband, Ryan, and three children, Layla, Gavin, and Madox, about my situation. I found out later that upon hearing the news, Gavin had responded, "We're not supposed to give Uncle Pat the cold shoulder, are we? Because he's our person. We love him."

Though my pain was excruciating and I felt nearly dead inside, Christmas gave me a glimmer of hope that I would get to experience far better Christmases in the future. At one point, John pulled me aside and quietly asked how I was doing. He and Rachel had lost their oldest daughter, Angie (Alesha's sister) to cancer when she was just twenty-four. Angie had been stunning, brilliant, and full of life. Her death left a scar that never faded.

If I had been in his shoes, I might've said something like, "Listen loser, I get that you're a screwup, but did you really need to drag my daughter and grandchildren down with you? I'm returning your presents, so why don't you crawl under a park bench where you belong?"

Fortunately, John was a far better man than I. John had seen hell, and somehow, he could see it in others too. John and I had an easy relationship over the years, but I can't say we were any closer than other fathers- and sons-in-law.

"It hurts, John," I said. "It fucking hurts so bad. I did this to my family. I did all of it."

He looked at me with quiet understanding and asked if I was thinking of hurting myself.

"Yes," I said, with tears rolling down my face.

"Promise me you'll call me if you're ready to act on those thoughts." He said it with a steely seriousness I'd never heard in his voice before.

I agreed.

Looking back now, I realize I was drowning in self-pity, so much so that I couldn't see the love all around me. And there was so much love.

The day after Christmas, I began obsessing over who ratted me out. Or, to use the vernacular I know this particular person would've used, I began obsessing over who "lodged a complaint" against me. But I knew immediately who'd done it: *Abrial.*

Objectivity is one of the most underrated virtues educators possess. I fell short in several areas during my educational tenure, but if someone asked me what I was most proud of as a teacher and administrator, I felt I acted in an impartial and unbiased manner toward every student, whether teaching or disciplining. It's important to evaluate each kid and each situation independently by stripping yourself of any bias or preconceived notion you may have toward them.

The assistant high school principal often polices the school, so I was an enforcer. I worked closely with Abrial, the juvenile court school liaison, who oversaw students involved in the juvenile court system, implemented and enforced discipline, and oversaw attendance and truancy.

Abrial was particularly good when searching a student for drugs, vapes, or weapons. She could read students' eyes as we searched, leading to hunches that often lead to contraband discovery in the most unusual and unlikely places. She viewed situations in a black-and-white manner, and could hold her own against the mouthiest of students. She and I became partners and formed an effective working relationship. In fact, data demonstrated that we reduced office referrals and increased attendance in an almost linear fashion until COVID-19 hit.

As a teacher, I learned fairly quickly that in teaching two hundred students and leading seven or eight different subjects, being flexible and forming relationships with students is vital. Sometimes you have to roll with the punches, challenge yourself to adjust and change, and most importantly, not to take things personally.

Abrial had never taught a day in her life. She was not a teacher and possessed no formal instructional education. I always felt that lacking this key classroom experience put her at a disadvantage in the work. While we typically saw eye-to-eye on most things, she seemed to take it personally when we disagreed on how to handle a situation. I felt like Abrial also held petty grudges against students if they disrespected her, and in no other way was this more evident than in her dealings with Eli, a frequent flyer in the high school office.

Eli had some behavioral issues and strong political opinions that weighed just right of Attila the Hun. Once he arrived at high school, he became entangled in multiple disciplinary situations, and everyone knew Abrial wasn't the best candidate to handle him. She all but recused herself from dealing with Eli, openly stating her disdain for the lad. Eli was smart and bloody clever. He possessed a comedian's sense of humor, and was just the kind of kid that could make you look like a fool if you let him.

So Eli became a project that fell to me, and my goal was to get him to graduate. Eli and I butted heads more than I did with any of our other young moral entrepreneurs, but at the end of the day, he was just another kid who'd had a rough life, and as a natural consequence, didn't trust adults. I spent time listening to him, which few adults in his life had taken the time to do.

The more time I spent with Eli, the more spiteful Abrial seemed. Cold comments and passive aggression replaced friendly chats and laughter.

Did she want him to fail? I couldn't let him; I was there to help kids, especially those who needed it most. Friendship, biases, grudges, and spite had no place in my territory.

So it is my belief that she hatched a well-laid-out plan to ensure the end of my professional career, and especially put a stop to the Eli work.

Did I have a problem with alcohol?
Absolutely.

Was this the best way for a friend and coworker to help?
I'm not sure.

Abrial left me no options, but her keen intuition likely led her to believe that only the greatest degree of corrective action would be effective.

Did she know that it might lead to my resignation?

I can't say. I'm not necessarily angry with her methods. After all, I was drinking alcohol and under its influence at my job and around students.

But I truly believe my work with Eli led her to act, and that hurts. To this day, I think of all of the students I tried to help in my twenty-three years in education. Several times during the months and weeks leading to that fateful day, I broke down in front of my students. My empathy for their pain, the absent parents, the troubled friendships, the abuse, the mental health issues, their despair so early in life—brought their pain and suffering directly to my heart as I myself was swimming against the current of my own addiction.

Once, a student in my office lashed out in anger as he had done so many times: "Life just freaking sucks and sometimes I just want to take a fistful of pills!"

I collapsed to my knees and wept in front of the student, who looked at me in shock. I just couldn't take these kids' anguish anymore. It had gotten to the point where every time a student opened up about their very real past traumas and current struggles, I felt an elephant sitting on my chest and hot coals in my brain. The student kneeled down next to me and asked if *I* needed a hug. Regardless of how things went down, I cherish every one of the kids that I tried to help. They were so worth it.

After Christmas, Mark, a friend of mine who was a year into his own recovery, stopped over one day. We made our way back to the sunroom behind my kitchen, where we could close the door and get into sobriety stuff. He offered a lot of good advice, and I finally found someone I could learn from and confide in. He mentioned that the rumor mill was buzzing. He didn't mention it as gossip, only that people love the drama and how selfish and foolish those who perpetuate it are.

He overheard someone saying, "Yeah, I guess he and the other principal were drinking cocktails all the time in the office, watching porn, and running some sort of escort service."

As he recalled it to me, he smiled slightly at the absurdity of it. However, he said he had interjected into this gossip, "You know, I know Pat, and I don't think you have your facts straight."

So there it was: I had become Jordan Belfort, The Wolf of Education.

For months after I lost my job, rumors bloomed like poppies, bright and dramatic. Rumors are rarely true; they are simply more interesting than the truth. The truth was anticlimactic: I drank, I unraveled, I got caught. There was no great Shakespearean tragedy, just a man in khakis who couldn't cope and reaped the consequences, but the hallways I used to stride through became corridors of speculation.

They didn't need facts, they needed a character, a cautionary tale for staff lounges and soccer moms. And unfortunately, when you collapse in public, people rearrange the wreckage into fast, dramatic, and intoxicating rumors that fit their worldview.

Thanks, Abrial. And yet, there's no sarcasm in my thanks. This was 100% my fault and I *should* feel ashamed. However, I wanted just one person to ask, "How did this happen?"—not for gossip, but for truth. Instead, I watched my name become shorthand for *failure*. The dull truth no one cares to hear is that there was no scandal, no big reveal, just a man who couldn't cope with what he had become.

On a cold Sunday afternoon in late December, I met Hutch at the high school to clean out my office. My friend Erik helped, and the air in the office hung heavy with dust and resignation. Erik stood beside me, his usual levity quieted as he helped stack papers and box up framed certificates that hadn't seen daylight in years. I peeled my nameplate off the door with a slow twist, the adhesive giving way without resistance.

Principal Hutch stood off to the side, arms crossed, his expression unreadable but unmistakably sad. He didn't speak much, just offered a few low murmurs when Erik made a joke or when we found an old student award. But his silence echoed louder than any farewell speech. Surprisingly, I felt nothing. No pang of nostalgia. No flare of regret. Just the dull mechanics of cardboard and tape as the room steadily emptied.

There was a scratch on the window frame where a student had once carved their initials during a crisis conversation. I ran my finger along it without thinking, like tracing the edge of a dear photograph. This office had been a refuge for kids on the edge—a place where tears were shed, futures wrestled with, and more than a few chairs kicked. I'd listened to confessions that never made it into files. Offered tissues to students who couldn't look me in the eye. Handed out second chances like lifelines. It had all happened here, in these four faded walls.

I realized the office never really felt like mine. The desk was always too big. The lighting was too dim. The air too still. It belonged more to the stories that unfolded than to me. It held the weight of kids who didn't think they mattered, and of kids who sometimes reminded me that I didn't, either. Erik taped the last box shut. Hutch still stood there, hands folded, eyes damp. There was no formal sendoff, no parting speech. He only offered the quiet understanding that this was how things end: not with applause, but with cardboard and silence.

I looked around one final time. I felt no swelling emotion. No grief. Just the strange emptiness of a chapter closing.

The door clicked behind us. I didn't look back.

Thanks, Abrial. Truly.

Chapter 5

Blue-Collar Grit and the Marine Corps / I Guess This is Growing Up . . .

"I have taken more out of alcohol than it has taken out of me."

—Winston Churchill

Pop psychologists like to pinpoint the reasons people become alcoholics: *Was it the mother? Was there a divorce? Was there a singular point in this drunken idiot's life that orchestrated his downfall?*

In other words, how the hell did all this happen? What brought Patrick Farley to this lowly state?

We, the *chosen*, the ones who more than likely have a preordained future with the Black Dog or whatever we choose to call our inner demonic muses, as we enter the maze of alcohol use. We often have a cognitive preoccupation with drinking. The science is complicated and far from conclusive. There is strong scientific evidence that addiction is rooted in our genetic makeup and in the way the brain's reward system operates. From a simplified neurobiological perspective, our brains *actually differ* from most people's. We have a condition known as hyperactive dopamine response, which means we release more dopamine, the "feel good" chemical, than the average person. Over time, our brains believe this surplus of dopamine means we don't need to produce as much, and it adapts to increase the level of dopamine transporters.

Can *anyone* develop an addiction? Probably. But for us, it's easier, fasttracked.

The alcohol must keep coming in at an ever-increasing volume necessary for this Frankenstein neural circuitry to continue to work, except. . . tiny problem. . . these volumes of alcohol start killing us. But *woe is he* should the alcohol cease to flow once these adaptations have taken place—to some, that's even worse than a slow death by bourbon.

Yes, cultural and social influences played a part in my alcohol use disorder (I'm okay with calling it alcoholism, by the way—many are not copacetic with that word), so yes, there is a genetic predisposition component to alcohol. Believe it or not, I did have the means to nip this thing in the bud and I failed. Or did I? This is a very contentious debate in medical circles.

A born-and-bred Midwesterner, I grew up in Iowa, where we luxuriated in hot summers playing baseball, breathed crisp fall air as we watched farmers harvest, hurtled down Hospital Hill on Flexible Flyers in the winter, and embraced rejuvenating, sweet air-scented springs.

Most kids think their families aren't all that different from anyone else's, and it's only through age and reflection that we gain an adult understanding of how things truly were, or at least probably were. I was the youngest, with two sisters. My sisters were both five and two years older than me, and we are still very close.

My father was an extremely hard worker; he owned and operated a small tire and auto repair business. We also sold cars. To this day, I can still smell the pungent grease on his hands mixed with the Ivory bar soap he used to clean himself up and the rubber of the tires in the store. It was a tantalizing aroma, and between that and the feel of the wrenches and other tools he kept in his shop, I was hooked at a young age. I started working at the store when I was six and worked there part time, off and on into my thirties.

I'll never forget one interaction between us in the shop. My dad was trying to get a rusted tire wheel off the hub assembly, but it was stuck. He tried prying it off with one hand and grabbing a tool to help him with the other, but couldn't quite reach. His dark hair, slicked with sweat, highlighted his narrow face. "Pat, grab me a pry bar or something to get this thing off."

I was about seven, and sprang into action, but in my inability to decide on the perfect tool for my dad, I ended up doing a little dance from one end of the shop to the other. I had to get *just* the right one.

"Pat!" Dad yelled, "now!"

"I'm trying, I'm trying," I yelped, before I grabbed the first thing I saw—an old, bent screwdriver, hardly the best candidate for the job.

"This is the best you could find?"

"Sorry, Dad." It was typical of the kind of conversation I had with him.

Our father loved us and worked extremely hard to provide. He loved us the best he knew how. He was stern and prone to mood swings, possibly because he had grown up as one of seven children from an Irish Catholic family and grew up defending his precious things, which included a collection of baseball cards his younger brothers frequently raided. He ran a tight ship and took a great deal of pride in his garden and landscaping. Like his yard, he insisted the house remain spotless.

I loved playing catch with Dad and my sisters, and we spent many summer evenings chucking baseballs across the side yard, where we faced less of a chance of hitting the house.

My mother's top priority was her kids. She loved being a mom, but living in the 1980s meant more families were becoming two-income homes as prices and interest rates rose. My mom attended nursing school at a nearby community college and became a registered nurse, providing much-needed secondary income to our family. We varied from a lower-middle-class to a middle-class existence, depending on how well my dad's business performed. I noticed that if his business was down, we ate chicken; if business was good, we ate steak.

Even so, we had enough food and clothes, joyful birthdays and holidays, and glorious summer vacations to what I thought were far-flung destinations: Wisconsin and Arkansas, with the occasional trip to the Ozarks.

My parents only drank socially; vacations and family get-togethers frequently featured beer and wine, occasionally liquor. Rarely did I see my mother get tipsy or my father have one too many beers, and neither have problems with alcohol now.

Adults occasionally gave me rare sips of beer and wine. I didn't understand the allure—it tasted bad, and liquor was even worse! The way grown-ups drank it in movies, I thought I was in for a real treat. Once, I stumbled on a few half-drunk bottles of whiskey and tequila, and I choked some down. It burned its way down my throat like poison. I remember thinking, "*Yeccchhh!* What's so great about this stuff?"

When I was ten, my parents lined up my sisters and me on the living room couch, in all its multifloral orange glory. Dad stood in the doorway with his arms crossed while Mom delivered the news. I watched her ball up a tissue in one hand as she said, "Your father and I," she faltered for a second, then exhaled hurriedly, "we're getting a divorce."

I watched my sisters' reactions. Their faces crumpled in an instant, tears flowing through their fingers.

"Why?" Sherie, my sister, practically screamed, "You're ruining our lives!"

My face felt normal, my feelings placid, as if they hadn't just delivered 9.5-on-the-Richter-scale news. I immediately sided with my father, and my sisters planted themselves with our mother—just a natural order of things, I guess. I'd like to say that my parents had a "good" divorce, but it was quite the opposite. They filled my early adolescence with custody battles, tumultuous visitations, and fighting—always fighting.

In the end, divorce teaches you that nothing is permanent. It turns family ties and familiar realities into little more than variables. The need for your family to stay together as a unit for a child is primal. When divorce comes, the family not only becomes fragmented, but you're also forced to decide how to divide weekends, holidays, birthdays, and time with each parent. Time and love almost become materialized. I believe this to be true, no matter how careful parents are with their divorce. It was certainly true of mine.

I now joke that my parents should co-author a book entitled, *What Not to Do When You Divorce*, but they'd never get along well enough to write it. The divorce was ugly, and my sisters and I often found ourselves right in the middle of the crossfire.

I would typically walk to my Dad's tire store after school to grab a snack and help out for an hour or two before helping him close the shop and go home for the day. About two to three months into the divorce, I was sitting in the waiting area, eating a Twinkie. It was close to closing time, and a lady was settling her bill with my dad, who was at the cash register.

My mother walked in and spoke to the lady before the woman left, just making small talk. My mom suddenly grabbed a new tire on display and stormed out the door. My dad had taken a few pieces of furniture from what used to be our house, but Mom apparently didn't agree to it. My father lurched over the desk, spit in her face, and they began wrestling, kicking, hitting, slapping, punching.

I curled my legs to my chin and screamed, "Stop it! Please guys, stop fighting!" I began crying hysterically. Verbal altercations between them were not uncommon, but this was different.

Choosing which parent to live with sucks. My sisters both declared they were staying with Mom; I felt a sense of obligation to stay with Dad. He took his tire business to Des Moines and soon got remarried to Connie, a widow with three sons: David, who was five; Jamie, who was thirteen; and Jon, who was eighteen. Looking back now, I believed I was happy. I had always wanted a brother, and now I had three. I largely put my mom and sisters out of my mind and went on with my new life in Des Moines. But attending St. Thomas of Aquinas in Webster City was quite different from the Des Moines public schools. I got into a lot of fights. It was like *Rocky V*, when Rocky loses his money and takes his family back to the Philly hood and his son gets beat up and learns how to fight.

I compartmentalized my new life in Des Moines and tried to forget my previous life in Webster City. I was enrolled in fifth grade at Watrous Elementary on the southeast side of Des Moines. I found it hard to make friends, and there was one lad in particular that constantly antagonized me. One day, he said something about my mom and I lost it.

Whoop, bang, pow, bam. I cried as I whaled on him, very much like Ralphie from *A Christmas Story*. After that, many kids left me alone and some even wanted to be friends. I took on a tough-kid persona, started listening to heavy metal, grew a sweet mullet, smoked cigarettes, took up skateboarding, and secured everything on my person with a trucker chain wallet. I bought a switchblade at a pawn shop near my dad's store, but luckily, I never had to use it. I was such a tough guy, and my dad was not impressed!

One day, I was working in the Des Moines tire store. I was around fourteen and working with a man who was a little rough around the edges, like a lot of my dad's employees. They were blue-collar street guys with nothing to offer the world but their labor. These men were broken. Life had kicked them in the face more than once, and they probably never received an ounce of love and support from home. Dad didn't have to pay them much, and there was a lot of turnover.

This guy, Ralph, had clear mental deficiencies. His coordination was poor, one of his eyes was cocked outward, and he was very slow to process information. He had some mechanical ability, though he was exactly the type of person who drove my Dad crazy. He was slow and different. My dad was hard on him; he yelled at him constantly. Ralph was an easy dog to kick.

I hated it. I felt so bad for the man, but what could I do? On this particular day, Ralph had jacked up a car and it slid off the frame, causing damage to the underbody of the car.

My dad lost it. "Get out of here! You're fired! Leave! Get out!"

Ralph just stood a few feet from the open bay door. He seemed confused, unable to process what was happening. My dad slammed the door to his office, but Ralph continued to linger. A few minutes later, Dad reentered the work area from his office. Ralph, still unaware of what had just happened, was still there.

"Get out of here! Leave!" Dad walked toward Ralph as if to intimidate him. Ralph, as if in a trance, got on his dilapidated ten-speed bike and slowly pedaled away. I hid behind a row of tires and couldn't fight back the tears. It was the saddest fucking thing I'd ever seen. Later in the afternoon, my dad confronted me. He must have seen his wimpy son scurrying from the scene.

"Do you think I was too hard on Ralph?" Dad asked.

"Yeah, Dad, he couldn't help it."

"No he's a loser, a liability to us. This is business, and if you're soft, it'll eat you alive. The sooner you learn that, the sooner you'll understand life. This isn't a charity, it's a business. Grow up!"

I guess I grew up.

We were a strong Catholic family. I guess as a kid I struggled to find where those teachings of kindness and charity stopped. So often in childhood, I experienced the opposite of what I heard on Sundays and what was drilled into me at parochial school. Heal the sick, be generous and kind to the needy—*unless they threaten the bottom line.*

I know my Dad is not the only businessman who operated under these paradoxes. Though for me, finding a moral compass and foundational virtues proved elusive. An unfinished and incomplete understanding of what "right" meant. The product: a childhood of uncertainty, questions with contradictory answers, an unprincipled youth.

After living with my dad, I ended up returning to my mom in her new role as sole custodian. I spent my teenage years with my mom, her husband, Dave, and my sister, who had a son named Curtis.

Did my parents' divorce cause my problems with alcohol? No, definitely not, but I will admit that I found just enough trouble to get into during high school, and our incidents often involved alcohol. I racked up a couple underage alcohol possession charges, which resulted in my mom saying, "Patrick, keys." She usually took my car away for about two weeks.

I didn't think much about alcohol until my teenage years—I noticed my family members drank, their friends drank, and of course, my peers almost all drank. I remember the first time I became inebriated.

I was thirteen.

I got my hands on some beer, drank six in about two hours, and threw up all over some guy's garage. I was with a few guys who were older than me. They patted me on the back as I held my head over a putrid-smelling garage drain. "Six beers? Not bad for thirteen!" I felt honored. I was *cool*—just one of the guys.

However, as I look back at my younger years, something seems a bit "off"—something odd and compulsive had wormed its way into my thinking. In particular, I remember some vivid, peculiar thoughts. For example, I remember watching a scene from the movie *Bram Stoker's Dracula*, with Anthony Hopkins as Dr. Van Helsing. In it, Van Helsing discusses the natures of vampires as he eats rare prime rib and chugs stout beer. My mom was also watching, and I asked her, "What's he drinking?"

"Beer," she responded. "In England, they enjoy it dark like that."

I remember thinking, "That looks really good. I bet it tastes delicious with a rare prime rib. I really want some of that."

I dismissed the fact that Van Helsing was discussing cutting a young lady's head off, or that he could transform into vapor, bats, or other humans. No, I was obsessed with the heavy consumption of dark English beer and how I might get my hands on some.

I was fourteen.

Houston, we might have a problem.

I began experiencing strange preoccupations when I watched people drink alcohol, though it wasn't frequent.

Middle school was strange. I fancied myself a tough kid from the Des Moines streets and had a huge chip on my shoulder. Though, the impact and work of teachers that truly care, and want to connect with students can never be understated. There was a young teacher named Kathy Davis who would often take me aside to attempt to connect with me. I took to her, and she made my middle school years a little less hectic. It doesn't always seem so at the time, though moments like that when you're a kid who feels alone, feeling the warmth of an adult truly caring about you, can be life changing. Kathy and I are friends today, and she has been a vital part of helping me through tumultuous times, just as she did when I was thirteen.

My freshman year in high school was a little rough. Bullying freshman was part of the norm at Webster City High School back in the nineties, though I came to love high school. It was not at all uncommon when I was a freshman to get punched in the hallway by upperclassmen for no reason whatsoever.

Once, my friend Erik, slid into his algebra class desk next to me, dripping wet from head to toe. He looked like a drowned, embarrassed rat.

"What happened?" I asked, aghast but suspecting the senior football players had nabbed him between classes.

Sure enough, he muttered, "They threw me in the shower." Erik ducked his head and opened his battered math book.

Times were different. It was difficult at first to return to Webster City after living with my dad in Des Moines, though I fell in love with the culture and traditions at Webster City High School. I found acceptance and an identity that had largely eluded me during the turmoil of custody exchanges and moving schools throughout fifth, sixth, and seventh grades.

Despite these skirmishes, I had a fantastic high school experience, earned average grades, played football and ran track, and was part of a great peer group and a good high school culture with enthusiastic teachers. I came into my own in high school and formed an identity.

I fell in love and had no idea what a romantic relationship was supposed to be. I didn't really know how to be a partner to someone. I suppose few teenagers do. The closer a girl would get to me, the more anger and resentment I built. My dad did not treat my mother well, nor did my stepfather. I had no real model as to how to love or treat a woman. I had a hard time opening up about my past, and would resort to wallowing in self-loathing if things in a relationship didn't go my way.

In the meantime, the military fascinated me. Like many late- post-Cold War, 1980s kids, I grew up watching war movies and playing with G.I. Joe action figures and a million of those little green army guys. Both of my grandfathers had served in World War II, most of my uncles had served, and my father was in the Army and National Guard for eight years. Sherie's husband Eric, a Sergeant First Class in the Army who deployed to Iraq. My cousin, Chuck, who was my role model as a teenager, was the one who really pushed me to join. Chuck entered the Marines and spent hours telling story after story about how difficult it was.

Undaunted, I made my decision to enter the Marine Corps when I was fourteen, because I thought becoming a Marine represented the pinnacle of adulthood. My dad thought I was an idiot for enlisting, which made me want to join even more. I enlisted in the spring of my junior year. One tranquil spring afternoon during my senior year, the reality of boot camp began to sink in.

I had an unusual, though not altogether unfamiliar, thought: "You know Pat, we like alcohol a lot. Someday, it'll likely become a problem. But if after or during the Marines we can get college educated and find some professional success, society might not judge us quite so harshly."

I was *eighteen* when I heard this prophecy, and strangely enough, it pushed me to take my early adulthood and career more seriously. Messed up, right? The idea that I might one day battle addiction actually motivated me to start making intentional, grown-up choices. Worst case scenario: *I'll be an educated drunk. That's not so bad.*

When I knew I wanted to enter the Marines, I took the Armed Forces Vocational Aptitude Battery (ASVAB), a standardized test to assess the aptitude of any potential recruit. I blew through the test and received a low score. I felt lower than low when I received my scores.

It was the first time I realized my dad's prophecies could actually come to fruition: I actually might turn out to be a failure.

"I'm stupid, Mom, and that's all there is to it," I said to her, crushing up the test, which revealed serious deficits in my verbal, math, science, and technical proficiencies.

My mom got a hard look in her eyes. Her brown hair shook a little in its puffy late-eighties style as she replied, "No, you're not. You just didn't focus! You *are* smart!"

My mom realized in her thirties that being a stay-at-home mom and housewife was not for her—she thought of cooking and cleaning and wiping snot as a "comfortable concentration camp" and longed for a profession. She put herself through nursing school, became a registered nurse, and launched her career, lovingly providing a second income to our beleaguered finances. Her professional journey provided the backdrop for guiding my sisters and me into careers as teenagers, so she immediately went out and purchased an ASVAB testing prep book for me. I worked tirelessly on it, and when I retook the ASVAB and quadrupled my score, the military thought I had cheated.

Nevertheless, the United States Marine Corps, including its thirteen weeks of grueling training provided me with a new identity and a sense of pride I had never before experienced. Becoming a Marine was and still remains one of the highlights of my life. It provided a catalyst to set goals and build a life worth living. I was driven to achieve.

My siblings, cousins, and other family members also wanted the best for me. Teachers and coaches challenged me to learn and achieve. Many in my life wanted me to find success and happiness. The late Dick Kennedy, who was the head wrestling and assistant football coach and who taught P.E. and health at the high school, had an enormous impact on me. He was a fantastic relationship-based teacher and coach who truly cared about "his kids." He motivated his students and players to put forth their best efforts. I lived with a lot of self-doubt, and he frequently encouraged me to fight past that thinking. Coach Dick Tighe was our head football coach and one of the top in the state. After playing for Dick, I coached alongside him for eight seasons. I truly benefited from his guidance, not only as an assistant coach, but as a young adult. It has been said that we spend our lives trying to either prove or disprove who we were in high school. I look back at my time as a student at Webster City High School with fondness, though the drink was an extremely stable factor in my younger years, and obviously would continue to be so as I entered adulthood.

Then there was my stepfather, Dave. I'm not sure Dave entirely knew what he was getting himself into by marrying my mother. When you marry a woman with children, you do probably need to take on somewhat of a parenting role. But Dave was an alcoholic who wanted little to do with being a father. Dave's personality and overall life outlook left him woefully unprepared for this role. Though it angered me to observe him stumbling around and yelling at my mother and sisters, I suppose I also learned that that is simply what men do: *They drink.*

Dave was an introverted mechanic, and with his average height, dark hair, beard, and burly build (complete with beer belly), he looked the part. He smoked a pack of unfiltered Camels a day and drank six to twelve Budweiser tallboys every night, sometimes adding a fifth of Black Velvet whiskey for good measure. (It's interesting how well I observed how much he drank every night.) Every night, he walked up the small stairwell of our split foyer house, a beer tucked in his armpit under his Carhartt coat.

"Hello," he sometimes muttered, but most of the time, he said nothing. He often made his way to his room only to disappear for the rest of the night. I suspect he was depressed, but my sisters and I didn't care; we didn't like this skulking stranger my mother seemed to tolerate. It didn't seem like the world's greatest romance, to say the least.

One summer back on leave from the Marines, I came home from a party late with my friend, Tyler, and we were both laughing loudly. Dave surfaced, smoking a Camel, clearly drunk, and said, "You guys need to shut the fuck up!"

I replied, "You don't need to talk to us that way. We're sorry."

He squared up to me. "You know what you are?"

"No."

He took a step toward me and repeated, "You know what you are?"

I shook my head, then added aloud, "I said no, you drunken imbecile."

"You're nothing but a pussy-ass Marine," he goaded, looking every bit like the sloppy loser he was.

"Would you like to step outside and see what kind of Marine I am?"

He swung at me, and it was on. We went at it hard, punching, pushing, wrestling, into the kitchen and living room, launching breakables, and at one point I hit him with one of Curtis's Tinker Toys. It was like a fight scene from *The Naked Gun*. I put Dave in a chokehold I learned in the Marines, and my mother and friend Tyler had to break us up.

Strangely, our relationship improved after the altercation. Dave was a deeply flawed man who had allowed alcoholism to penetrate his psyche. His body was also beaten down by his daily work as a mechanic; he sported a badly torn shoulder and slipped discs in his back. Dave and I worked on cars together, grilled, drank beer, and became friends throughout my twenties. Sadly, Dave lost his job, succumbed to alcoholism, and died of cirrhosis in 2010 at the age of forty-six.

Ironically, I was about his age when I lost *my* job. Were our fates aligned?

Many can contribute stories about exploits with alcohol in early adulthood. I partied in every sense of the word: at keggers, in bars, Friday After Class (FAC) and Thirsty

Thursdays in college, during my twenty-first birthday, road trips, concerts, spring breaks . . .

In high school, we drank cheap beer and vodka. It was ingrained in the culture of small-town Iowa as much as we Iowans grew and harvested corn. When I wasn't training in the Marines, I was probably drinking. I branched out into mixed drinks, craft beers (which I grew to love), and learned how to sip whiskey and other libations. As I recall all the impaired memories in the thick of my partying days, it was fun to let the drinking take the nights where they would go—and someday, it would dictate the days as well.

Alcoholism, or alcohol use disorder, advances in stages. (Again, I don't get caught up in the politics of the terms "alcoholic," "addict," "alcohol use disorder," etc. It's all the same. I call myself an alcoholic.) We'll go with the four-stage model, because it makes the most sense to me:

- Stage 1: Alcohol use
- Stage 2: Misuse
- Stage 3: Abuse
- Stage 4: Addiction

No two alcohol addiction paths look the same. My stages looked like this:

- Stage 1: Alcohol use: Teen years

- Stage 2: Misuse: Teen years
- Stage 3: Abuse: Late twenties
- Stage 4: Addiction: Thirties and forties

I was at stage one and two in my teens, which involves experimentation and social drinking. As I entered my early twenties, my tolerance definitely began to increase. Alcohol became more and more present in my life. At that point, alcohol was largely reserved for weekends and one or two weeknights if the occasion called for it. By my late twenties, I was definitely entering stage three. I consumed alcohol daily or near daily. Efforts to moderate were challenging. I built up more tolerance and found myself frequently intoxicated. I found myself counting the minutes until I could have a drink after work and counted down past noon on the weekends.

After the Marines, I studied history, psychology, economics, and political science and earned an education degree from the University of South Dakota. I'd always had a passion for history, and teaching seemed a natural career pursuit. My career goal was never to become rich; wealth accumulation didn't interest me. I had just enough interest in my classes to keep the balance—decent grades, steady work, and a social life that ran hot every Thursday through Saturday at bars, tailgates, and happy hours. Drinking made me feel good—euphoric, untethered, free. It wasn't just part of the scene; it *was* the scene.

Whether I was in Vermillion or reconnecting with the old high school crew in Cedar Falls, Ames, or Iowa City, alcohol was always the centerpiece. Beer, mixed drinks, shots—it didn't matter. What mattered was the buzz, the belonging, the illusion of control. And for a while, I managed it. I worked part-time, sometimes full-time. I kept my grades up. I showed up. I balanced the party with the performance.

Until the balance tipped.

One night, I got arrested for fake ID possession. It was supposed to be just another night out, complete with cheap drinks, loud music, the usual blur. But that ID, that little laminated lie, was the first real crack in the façade. I remember the cold fluorescent lights of the station, the way time slowed down as they processed me. The officer's voice was flat, almost bored, but the moment felt seismic. I wasn't just a college kid with a party habit, I was now a number in a system, a cautionary tale in the making.

It should've been a wake-up call. But instead, I treated it like a fluke. A hiccup. I minimized it, rationalized it, buried it under bravado. I told myself I was unlucky, not unraveling. But looking back, that arrest was a turning point. Not because it stopped me, it didn't. But because it marked the moment when alcohol stopped being a choice and started becoming a requirement. It eventually would no longer ask for moderation. It would demand total allegiance.

My mother, a nurse, preached that the highest virtue is to help people, and this notion became central to my life philosophy. My father's tire store had taught me the value of hard work, and high school sports taught me invaluable teamwork skills and perseverance. I began building the beginnings of a cherished life that I would later ruin.

I was also extremely immature. I went through periods of sloth and apathy, and alcohol was often a culprit. One day in philosophy class, something shifted. Dr. John Fremstad, my favorite professor, the kind of thinker who could make abstract ideas feel personal, asked me to present an essay I'd written on John Stuart Mill and utilitarianism. I wasn't expecting it. But as I stood in front of the class, something clicked. I came alive. The ideas weren't just words on a page anymore—they were mine. I spoke with clarity, conviction, and a rhythm that felt natural, almost electric. I could see it in the room: students leaning in, smiling, nodding. Some were surprised. Maybe I was, too. I wasn't the guy with the fake ID anymore. I wasn't just the one who could balance the party with the grades. At that moment, I was a teacher. A guide. A voice. I found a knack. A calling. It was more than academic it seemed, almost spiritual! The philosophy of Mill, with its focus on the greatest good for the greatest number, mirrored something I hadn't yet named in myself: a desire to serve, to elevate, to connect. That day planted a seed, but it didn't bloom immediately. There were still years of detours, distractions, and darker chapters ahead. But the memory of that moment, of coming alive in front of others, of being seen and heard, stayed with me. It became a compass.

I fell in love with teaching. Other teachers, professors, (and soon administrators), seemed to take note that I had a knack for reaching and working with at-risk kids.

As I look back on this period of my life, I remember Japanese Admiral Yamamoto's quote after their attack on the U.S. Navy Fleet at Pearl Harbor: "I fear all we have done is to awaken a sleeping giant and fill him with a terrible resolve." It was the same with my burgeoning relationship with alcohol. Together, we would set sail on a progressive course toward disaster.

Years of studying and teaching psychology have taught me that human behavior is rarely driven by a single cause. An inborn obsession with drinking, the pull of family and social influences, and the wounds of childhood turmoil all joined to plant a seed that grew into poison and thorns. Many had it far worse than I did, but make no mistake: The seed of anguish is often planted in childhood, and I am no exception.

Sadly, alcohol provided a tangible pleasure that motivated me to pursue success into early adulthood. In the back of my head, I thought I'd always have it to turn to as a special euphoria to buffer against life's perils, come what may.

Note: I began this chapter with a quote from Churchill. I don't know if Sir Winston himself was ever addicted to alcohol. Probably—it was a different time. Ironically, I took refuge in his words because it was useful as a rationalization for my drinking. However, I believe his wisdom regarding alcohol is somewhat incomplete. Here's what he should've said: *"We take more out of alcohol than it takes from us. That is, until one day, we do not."*

Chapter 6

Cakes/When a Woman Loves a Man

"Simply put, I love her in ways that I don't even
know about yet."

—Journal entry, December 2007

Do you want to know how to test a marriage?

Here's a great recipe: Add an embarrassing
and public humiliation to your family's
reputation. Yes, squander any esteem that your
family name might hold. Now, subtract a
twenty-three-year career culminating into a
six-figure income. Subtract your social life.
Next, deduct your professional state licensures
and credentials that you beat the odds to earn.
Mix with ongoing symptoms of physical and
psychological withdrawal from alcohol. Lastly,
add just a dash of inability to show up as a
husband and a father due to alcohol addiction
withdrawal, and there you have it. *Voilà!*

When you're married, you sometimes meet
people other than your spouse with whom you
have stronger mutual interests: a similar sense
of humor, common interests, identical favorite
foods, and more. And that's fine. It's important
to maintain friendships in addition to your
marriage and meet new people. However, I've

found that the initial love and passion in early marriage evolves into a bond.

Marriage is about having someone who will bear witness to your life—the good and the bad, and provide unconditional support when you fall. Love is a feeling of someone being there, a warmth forged by more than just mutual interests and lust. Even the most compatible partners will fail if the bond isn't there.

I believed my wife would forget about her unconditional love for me after I wrecked everything. Marriage is hard work, and though Alesha was my partner and I loved her, I thought that if the going got tough, Alesha would get going. It probably had a lot to do with my parents' divorce. Nothing was sacred, even a promise to love each other forever—it's what my parents had unintentionally beat into my head.

Alesha and I both attended Webster City High School. She was a freshman when I was a senior, but despite the age difference, we hung out in the same circles and shared many of the same friends. After high school, we worked together briefly at a theater and did not particularly care for each other. She claims I avoided work and did not help out enough; I say I didn't want to be around her and her gossipy friends, so I worked mostly solo. Our personalities were then (and still are) very different. I guess opposites really do attract.

After breaking up with my fairly serious girlfriend in my mid-twenties, I wasn't sure I wanted to get right back into a relationship, so I played the field—a girl here, a girl there, nothing serious. One night, I was out having dinner and drinks with some friends at the Saloon, a popular bar and grill in Webster City. In 2005, it was a bit of a dive, but it sold great food and strong drinks. The prices varied depending on how much the manager, Steve, liked you, and my tickets generally hit the middle range. The Saloon had a wide open seating area, so you could clearly see who was coming and who was going.

As I took a large sip of my dark beer, I noticed a striking blonde: Alesha Norem. She walked by without noticing my friends and me at all. She had always been one of the most beautiful young ladies in high school, and now as a young woman . . . *Wow. Blonde hair, green eyes, perfect figure.*

I usually looked past this type of girl. *Too much work,* I thought.

At this point, Heather, a friend of mine from high school who was with us, leaned over her bar stool and said, "I think Alesha Norem's single."

A nice thought, but no way. I didn't think she'd be interested, nor did I think we'd have much in common. But she was so beautiful, and I rationalized that we had been a lot younger when we couldn't stand each other at the movie theater.

I didn't have the courage for an all-out ask: "Wanna go out for dinner sometime?" so I took the coward's way out. My mom was friends with a woman whose daughter was friends with Alesha. I asked my mom to put a feeler out to see if Alesha would be at all interested in a date. *What a chicken I was!*

My contact said she was agreeable to a date, so I gave her a call. I still remember our first date and how wonderful she looked.

Could I really make her mine?

Since February 2005, Alesha has been by my side. We fell in love, like *madly* in love. We couldn't get enough of each other. I married my Alesha when I was twenty-nine. We've worked hard to build a marriage we've never given up on. We are partners in the truest sense of the word, and that beats all the Shakespeare in the world. She has been by my side for nearly twenty years now, providing us with two beautiful children, plus our niece, Chelsey, who has lived with us for six years.

After we married and she completed a registered nursing degree, we acted on a desire to take our careers and family outside our hometown, so we moved our family around the state. We created beautiful homes for our children, built our careers, and one highlight was taking on head varsity football jobs. I helped turn previously winless teams into playoff qualifiers. Our marriage, like many, had highs and lows. Somehow, she kept our family together and by my side, but if I'm honest, this is the fairy tale version.

A deeper look tells the story of two young adults with gaping emotional wounds from childhood and adolescence. We're both the youngest children in our families with different personalities and interests whose values and family upbringing contrasted.

We fought. And bickered and picked at each other and even conspired against each other. In the summer of 2011, we separated, and our marriage hung by the thinnest thread more than once. In 2009, we picked up and moved from a beautiful house we loved in larger-city Ames, Iowa, to a rental in small town Vinton, Iowa. Alesha came home to a small house, her life in boxes, in a town where she didn't know a soul, while I put every ounce of my energy into teaching and into coaching a previously winless football team. Furthermore, I was not great at caring for her and Boston, who was a newborn. Being a coach's wife is stressful, especially when things are not going well for the team. This additional stress was the last thing she needed in a foreign town with a newborn, on top of her persistent sadness and anxiety. As a result, she had difficulty finding footing in what seemed like a whole new world, and new baby. Later we recognized she was suffering terribly from postpartum depression.

Did alcohol play a part?

Absolutely. I was well into my abuse stage. I didn't drink every night, but I drank most nights. I made friends with other teachers and coaches and we hit up bars. I remember thinking my drinking was not all that different from the other guys'.

Alesha's relationship with alcohol was very different from mine. Though I drank a lot, my personality didn't change much while under the influence. I could usually function just fine with a lot of alcohol sloshing around in my bloodstream. However, this contrast in drinking styles and gradual move toward dependence definitely didn't escape Alesha. She did *not* like the amount I drank. She didn't care for the fact that virtually every occasion (and often no occasion at all) was anchored in drinking.

"Pat, don't you think you've had enough?" She'd ask.

"Enough what?" I'd respond, cracking open another delicious IPA. "I can switch to bourbon," I'd say, grinning like an idiot. I always felt just a touch cleverer (and I hoped, cuter in Alesha's eyes) with a few drinks under my belt. There was a time when anything that threatened my drinking, no matter how innocent or well-intentioned, felt like an intrusion. A hike on a Sunday morning, a dinner with friends who didn't drink, even a spontaneous road trip that might take me too far from my usual supply. I'd meet these suggestions with a quiet recoil, a subtle but unmistakable disdain. Not loud enough to spark a fight, but my wife noticed. She always did.

She'd offer up plans with a hopeful lilt, watching my face for signs of resistance. And when it came, when I hesitated, deflected, or flat-out declined, her expression would shift. Not into anger, but something softer and more painful: disappointment. A kind of sadness that didn't ask for apology, just acknowledgment.

She never said, "You chose drinking over me." She didn't have to. It hung in the air between us, unspoken but undeniable. I could feel it in the way she stopped suggesting things. She started making plans without me. In a way, her laughter grew quieter, like she was rationing it.

Looking back, I realize it wasn't the drinking itself that hurt her most, it was the way it rearranged my priorities. The way it made her feel like an afterthought. Like joy, spontaneity, and connection had to compete with a bottle.

I didn't mean to push her away, but I did. Not with cruelty, but with neglect. And that kind of wound, the slow erosion of trust and intimacy, leaves scars in the pauses of conversation and in the way someone stops reaching for your hand.

When we were younger, we experienced strained finances: daycare, diapers, doctor visits, formula: the costs of life added up faster than we could count. Our marriage seemed to evolve into an uneasy peace. We went months without fighting, then would suddenly erupt into a volatile argument. We cried, then had sex. Sex wasn't much of an issue; we truly did love each other. Though, sex when you're struggling with alcohol dependence is just weird and often not very good. Sometimes it works, sometimes it doesn't' it's just sort of a mess.

One day in August 2011, the house was quiet. Unnaturally quiet. I had just come back from football practice, still damp with sweat and the hum of adrenaline, expecting the familiar sounds: Boston tossing something across the living room, Tessi humming a tune off-key, Alesha somewhere in the kitchen calling out for me to wash up before dinner, but when I opened the door, the silence met me like a wave. There were no backpacks by the door, no shoes scattered across the rug.

There was no laughter, only stillness.

My heart couldn't figure out if it was broken or just stunned. She *left*. She took the kids and left. And so I turned to what was still sitting on the shelf, still cold in the fridge, still whispering familiarity. The Black Dog didn't judge me. Didn't demand answers. It was the only thing that felt like family in that moment—predictable, present, and destructive. I poured a drink, convincing myself it was just to take the edge off. Then another. Then another. And with each one, the emptiness blurred.

She came back in the fall. Eventually, we drew certain boundaries with each other without words, and our marriage functioned, though I'm sure it could have been better in about a million different ways. When you're an alcoholic, you lose emotion. You live in a constant state of delusion and turmoil, self-love is impossible, and connection with others is difficult. I was constantly waiting for Alesha to pull the trigger, kick me to the curb, take the kids, and start anew.

On December 8, 2023, Alesha became one of my only beacons of hope.

I'm certain Alesha contemplated leaving for good. If I were her, *I* would've left me. But she says the thought never really surfaced. I keep a journal in which I write infrequently. It's probably the best timeline indicator of when my drinking transitioned to physical dependence. I simply stopped writing, or instead, scribbled a few notes of self-hatred. However, one day, I described how Alesha would absolutely leave me should I ever self-destruct.

But she didn't leave. *She fought alongside me.* As I dug into my psyche, I realized that fear of abandonment remained an unresolved conflict due to my parents' divorce, which fueled my alcoholism and presented significant barriers in my ability to be an effective husband. This revelation would surface along with many others as I took on my own demons. I cannot remember the source, though I remember reading that marriage is a promise to disconnect and connect with a person so many times that trust is established. It's the ultimate course in personal growth. It is not a promise that you will always be happy.

Alesha came to know the worst thing about me. She knew my deepest, darkest secret that I lied, deceived, and hid for years in shame. She linked arms with me and guided me anyway. How she found the love, inner strength, loyalty and devotion to keep our family together I will never know. I recently asked her how she did it. She looked at me with those big green eyes. "*I* didn't. *We* did," she said.

My Dearest Darling Cakes,

It's been a whirlwind the last 40 or so days hasn't it... There are times when I take measure of all that has happened and wonder if I'm dreaming. I've essentially traded my career for sobriety, a bitter sweet exchange. I look back at my 23 years of experience and education, and pray I can salvage them in some capacity. Know that I will do everything I can to put whatever I can together to provide for our family.

I could care less about my reputation/image in the community. Yes there is some shame and embarassment, but I have thick skin and have never really concerned myself with what the public thinks of me; especially WC gossipers. What does cause me heartache and sadness is the cloud that now follows you and the kids. I've jeopardized the integrity of our family and I fear you and the kids may bare the brunt of it. Know that I'm so very sorry for this. I truly never meant to hurt anyone.

Two big surprises have occured to me involving us/you. ① I didn't realize you still loved me so much. ② You have a strength and steadfastness in time of crisis that I've been leaning on heavily. I also saw this in you when you confronted Brady. I love you so much and cannot express enough gratitude for standing by my side. This thing grew and grew and like a virus, used my own mechanisms against me. I was too weak to stop ultimately.

120

So, Now it's back to Square One in a way. My top priorities are to be the best Husband + Father I can be, and provide the best I can for the lovely family + Home that we built. Please <u>KNOW</u>, I traded so much damage, loss, and Carnage for Sobriety. The Sobriety is now mine, and to give it back means that all of the above was sacrificed in vain. That I hurt you all for nothing. This I will never do. I love you. I love our kids. I will keep fighting.

Truly Yours,

Patrick

Letter I wrote to Alesha in January 2024 while in treatment to try to offer what little reassurance I could.

Chapter 7

Decline and Disillusionment

"If most of us remain ignorant of ourselves, it is because self-knowledge is painful and we prefer the pleasures of illusion."

—Aldous Huxley

I loved the way alcohol made me feel, and I knew people liked being around me when I drank. My personality came alive like an ember stoked into a raging fire. I was quick in conversation, met and connected with new people easily, and generated ridiculous ideas that I believed to be novel and intellectually unique. I laughed and laughed. Drunken humor became hysterical with the right company.

Everyone knows someone who is a drunk, an alcohol addict. It's nothing special, yet alcohol's great slyness infiltrates the ego. Like a parasite, it replicates itself with our own mental DNA. Despite all the warnings and messages out there about its danger, it becomes our religion. And let me tell you, we are a devout bunch.

So when did the bad stage (Stage Four) *truly* start?

Good question. I learned firsthand the difficulty in looking back to try to decipher the truth versus alcohol-induced misperceptions and delusions. It's easy to look back and say, "Oh, that bad thing happened because of alcohol."

In other words, could I attribute my behavior to *me* or the alcohol?

During college, many of us party like rock stars. Once most of us move into "the real world," we downshift from party mode into adulthood. Others continue the party lifestyle alongside their careers, marriage, family, etc. I would be willing to bet that if an expert conducted a study on this, they'd find that many of us who begin struggling with alcohol in midlife share some form of predisposition to alcohol use disorder, but I still remind myself constantly: I made my own choices as the scenery on my roadmap became darker and darker.

I do recall being mostly happy throughout my twenties and into my thirties. My life was balanced and my star seemed on the rise. I was still *me*. Sounds strange, I know, but when the balance of occasional drinking tips over into problem drinking and addiction, you literally lose yourself. Much of our consciousness, memory, and perceptions provide us with identities, beliefs, opinions, preferences, joy, sadness, etc. Once you cross the bridge into addiction, these things become subject to alcohol, and you are no longer you.

Another key challenge: literally thousands of people, places, events, vacations, getaways, are directly linked to alcohol. For example, in my mid-twenties, I spent a month in London, and one evening found me on the patio of an old English pub just off Piccadilly Circus. I drank a pint, watching the blur of city life, when a man who looked strikingly like me approached and asked if he could sit down. He was English, my age, and—oddly enough—a teacher too. We formed an instant connection.

We talked about education, philosophy, and politics as we drank pint after pint. The conversation was rich and engaging, the kind that makes the hours slip by unnoticed. Eventually, I muttered, half to myself, "I'm starting to do this too often."

He raised his glass with a smirk. "Alcohol is the anesthesia by which we endure the operation of life," he said. "That's Shaw, lad. Cheers," he said.

That line stuck with me too well. It became a quiet creed, tucked into my mental pocket like a justification, a bit of pub-born wisdom I could pull out whenever another round felt too indulgent. *We do that, don't we? We dip philosophy in liquor and hold it up as gospel, turning clever quotes into permission slips.*

But somewhere between inspiration and repetition, the ritual twisted. Eventually, quotes couldn't hide the truth anymore. The philosopher's wisdom would become the addict's excuse.

Alesha put together a party for me when I completed my master's degree. At that time, we had a beautiful little house with a quaint patio area off a small flower garden with a brick walkway. She had arranged for a full bar on a rolled-out oak vendor cart, complete with a stainless steel bucket of ice, martini shakers, and the other fun add-ins that helped us feel like sophisticated drinkers. We also sprung for a keg of ice cold red Irish beer on that gorgeous spring day. My mind remembers events like my master's degree celebration and wants to recreate them. It says, "When are we going to do that again?"

We're not. Never . . . not a possibility. This line of thinking, along with thousands of other memories, recollections, and experiences with alcohol, must be reframed in order for sobriety to work. I had a great time with alcohol. It was fun as hell until the end, when it turned on me.

Back to Stage Four. At certain points while I was teaching, I knew I was headed for trouble. It was getting more and more difficult to get to early evening without a drink. I also experienced anxiety, headaches, and at times, slight tremors and sweating.

Here's a terrible irony: Early in my teaching career, I was a substance abuse prevention specialist. In 2003, I took a certification workshop at Eastern Kentucky University, where the curriculum centered around the brain and addiction. I absorbed an enormous amount of information on the pathways of addiction, especially alcohol addiction. I read guidelines about the quantity and frequency of alcohol consumption based on genetic predisposition markers.

At that point, I was drinking sporadically. I might go weeks without drinking, though I drank a lot when I *did* drink. I was shocked to learn that at that consumption level, I was at risk for developing dependence. The guidelines suggested I drink two to three fewer drinks daily to keep alcoholism at bay, so I tried to adhere to those "rules" in my mid-twenties. I also took a month off from drinking once per year. I was aware of the science behind addiction, and was determined to manage its burgeoning blossom. *But addiction fucking crept in anyway.* Soon the month off from drinking became unrealistic, so I'd teeter back and forth.

I'd think, "Perhaps it's the hard liquor that's making me want to drink all the time, so I'll just drink beer." (And then proceed to drink seventeen beers a day.)

Then I'd say to myself, "Beer has a lot of carbonation and calories. I'm gaining weight and having bad hangovers, so let's just do vodka and Diet Sprite."

The vodka and Diet Sprite worked! I was drinking most of the bottle, leaving an ounce or so. *See, no drinking problem, lots of people have drinks after work, as long as it's not a whole bottle.* But then the ounce was no longer spared and I'd get mad at the bottles. Those stupid little bottles.

I know! These bottles are too small. I'll get bigger bottles. Problem solved, plus, I'll save money! The 1.75-liter handles are cheaper per ounce. Eureka! Moderation obtained, problem solved!

Ten years prior to being driven home by my superintendent, I was living in Marshalltown, Iowa, teaching history, psychology, and government at East Marshall High School. I was also the head varsity football coach. My drinking was well underway to becoming completely out of control. At this point, I had taught and coached for thirteen years. As my tolerance built, I could usually avoid hangovers with vitamins, fish oil, and water. I drank moderately to heavily every night. By Sunday, I usually drank from mid-morning throughout the rest of the day.

I truly knew I was headed for trouble when I couldn't get excited about Christmas unless I was drinking, because as I shared earlier, I love Christmas! My thoughts during the early stages of drinking: *Oh, we can mix rum with eggnog, and there are those yummy dark flavored beers, and winter wine! How festive!*

Then one day I came home after work, saw the tree with its lights, tinsel, and my ornaments (I've collected Hallmark ornaments since 1998—I have a collection approaching a thousand. I know I'm a freak. I need help—maybe after I conquer booze!). I saw the presents under the tree, the candles, all of the things that usually put a smile on my face because it was Christmas.

The joy didn't spark like usual. I wanted a drink. Only then could I sit back and enjoy Christmas in a chemically altered state. The Black Dog had successfully infiltrated Christmas!

One Sunday evening in the spring of 2015, I drove my blue Trailblazer to the grocery store not far from my house to purchase a gallon of milk. I had been drinking all day and decided to grab a twenty-four-ounce beer at a gas station. I was close to home but planned to chug the remainder of the beer before walking in the front door.

I noticed a car on my tail in the rearview mirror. *A police cruiser.*

Its red and blue lights whirred on. I had been pulled over in the past with alcohol in the car, mostly as a teenager.

Typically, anxiety and fear kicked in, but not this time. I felt *relieved*. Maybe I was super inebriated. But as I look back, I don't think so, because I distinctly remember a voice in my head said, "Good, now we'll get caught, charged with an OWI, go to jail, and the Black Dog will die."

I slowly pulled into the small driveway of an insurance agency. The officer sped past me, probably on the way to a different incident. It's difficult to explain the commingled euphoric relief and disappointment I felt.

Would this consequence have changed my trajectory?

I don't know.

Confused emotions were at the heart of my alcoholic experience. It was a tangled web of guilt, denial, fear, hope, shame, and longing that rarely followed a straight line. Alcohol was both my escape from pain and the source of it, keeping me from emotional clarity.

A voice in my head knew there was a problem. Sadly, that voice would be largely muted for ten years.

Chapter 8

The Answer (Ha!) to My Problems: The Naltrexone Spiral

"Do you really think; that I would ever let you go?"

—*Hyde, from the musical Jekyll & Hyde*

Okay, now I think I'm starting to have a problem.

Between the ages of approximately thirty-five to forty-two, I descended into addiction. If hell is the impossibility of reason, then drinking, as it wove ever deeper into my life, became my own private hell.

As addicts, we don't really know or understand it when it happens, but once addiction begins to take hold, we enlist loved ones to support our addictions. In fact, we manipulate those that have an interest in stopping our self-destruction. So we displace, we spin, we sublimate, we lie. We do whatever is necessary to create an environment fertile for the addiction to flourish, or at the very least, survive. It's like a cancer that creates the perfect breeding ground with which to wrap its tentacles around the next organ.

This process was well under way as my babies became children and I made my way toward middle age. The drinking got worse. In my mid-thirties, I used the stress of fatherhood and career as an excuse to drink to excess. I drank most nights and had benders on the weekends, usually starting in the morning. In my twenties, I might have only drunk in the morning during an Iowa State football game or some other outing where morning drinking felt somewhat socially acceptable.

If something wasn't socially acceptable, my attitude became, "Well then, let's make it so!"

It became ridiculous. I'd wake up on a Saturday or Sunday morning praying that I'd catch a football game in Europe, Mexico—really, anywhere. As long as football was on, the drinking would be sport-related and would therefore only slightly defy conventional norms. Slight drinking deviations were a key feature of my alcoholism. Bowl game season was the best—there are so many bowl games now. Any Division, any level would do: "Yes! Presbyterian College Blue Hose vs. Wagner College! Break out an eighteen-pack!"

Try as I might, I could not hide my problem from Alesha. I made excuses, talked about my love of craft beers as a hobby, etc. But she couldn't turn a blind eye to the problem that was beginning to boil over: empty bottles piled up (not the small ones), constant napping, the smell of alcohol constantly on my breath, strange mannerisms and nonverbals, etc. Loved ones of the addicted compile much data over time, learning to sense when the affected person is using: a slight stagger, dryness of the mouth, different speech patterns, a quiet that becomes a loud tell.

Alesha's database was starting to become quite intuitive and she was growing tired of it. I knew that the drinking was getting out of hand, though I was light years away from wanting to stop. She rarely confronted me with fury. That wasn't her style. Instead, she'd ask gentle questions that felt like scalpel cuts—precise, quiet, and hard to ignore: "Are you tired or just foggy?" or, "Did you eat today, or was that just beer again?" Her tone was soft, but the subtext was sharp. She was mapping patterns, tracking inconsistencies, building a case not for court, but for clarity.

And I knew it. I'd counter with charm, with deflection, with the kind of practiced ease that only comes from years of hiding. I'd wax poetic about hops and fermentation, about the artistry of small-batch brewing, as if that could mask the fact that I was drinking to disappear, not to appreciate. My hobby had become a disguise, and she saw through it.

The house began to feel like a crime scene, with evidence everywhere. The recycling bin clinked like a confession. My breath, my posture, my sudden silences—they all testified. And Alesha, unwillingly deputized, became the investigator of a life unraveling in slow motion. She didn't want the job. She wanted her husband back.

But I was slipping into naps that weren't restful, into moods that weren't mine, into a version of myself that felt increasingly foreign. I knew the slope was steep, but I wasn't ready to climb out. Not yet. The bottle still felt like a friend, even as it betrayed me.

How could I get back to moderation?

My friend Google offered a potential solution: A drug named naltrexone and a treatment known as the Sinclair Method surfaced. *There it was! A scientific solution to my problem!*

I became instantly excited. However, this meant I would have to go to an internist and state I was having problems with alcohol, which didn't excite me.

But maybe the drug would allow me to continue to drink *and* I'd get a handle on my powerful cravings! *Maybe I could have my cake and eat it too?* There's a fantastic TED Talk I watched in which a delightful woman who struggled with her drinking took on the naltrexone remedy and cured her addiction. I was sold!

I wiped my hands on my shorts and caught Alesha in the kitchen late one night (after a few beers, of course). "Hey, babe. I've been thinking lately that I really don't . . . Well, I think I've been drinking a little too much lately," I faltered. "I'd . . . I'd like to talk to a doctor about a treatment I've been looking into."

She was so happy to hear these words, as if she had been praying for them. "I'm proud of you Pat, I'll make the appointment," she said.

We went to a doctor in Marshalltown, Iowa, who prescribed naltrexone. I was somewhat surprised that she mentioned naltrexone can reduce cravings, yet she didn't seem willing to discuss—or perhaps didn't know—about the technique you should use when taking the drug.

Here's how the Sinclair Method works in a nutshell: When you drink alcohol, dopamine is released, which makes us feel good. Naltrexone is an opioid blocker designed for those overdosing on an opioid drug like percocet and heroin. Dr. David Sinclair theorized that if you take naltrexone with alcohol, it would prevent the brain from releasing the dopamine. In other words, you drink and you don't get the desired effect/chemical reward. Instead, you may become tired and your nervous system will still be impaired or slowed, but you don't get a buzz. Over time, you become conditioned to recognize alcoholic beverages as "just another beverage." The cravings slowly cease, and drinking becomes somewhat normalized. The combination of neuropharmacological and behavioral psychology joins forces to decondition your dependent or near-dependent brain using a blended approach of neurobiological pharmacology and behavioral psychology.

Imagine Pavlov recreating his experiment, except the dog receives a drug blocking the desire for food. Over time, the dog would not associate the sound of the tuning fork with the food. The salivation response would cease.

This could be it.

It worked. Sort of. In an *A Clockwork Orange* kind of way.

I drank my usual amounts, maybe a bit less, and I definitely did notice the lack of neural pleasure—I simply became tired while drinking. After about three to four weeks, my desire to drink did begin to diminish. I began taking alcohol-free days, and my cravings lessened. They weren't gone, however. I was proud that I could take it or leave it. I was still preoccupied with alcohol. I certainly had no desire to cut it out completely, but I could put a leash on it.

But here's one problem with the Sinclair Method: There isn't enough research on what happens when people drink alcohol without naltrexone after using it for a long time. Once, halfway home from a weekend in Clear Lake, my mind froze. "Oh shit! I forgot my naltrexone!" I said to Alesha.

In the back of my mind, I remembered a researcher saying, "Woe is he who drinks alcohol without naltrexone after utilizing the Sinclair Method."

When I arrived home, I pondered drinking without it. I decided that I would probably be okay and I would get some new naltrexone later on. I poured a Red Bull and vodka in the afternoon.

My God, if there's a heaven, this is what it must feel like.

The euphoria of the drink and the drinks to follow that day felt like I had just slept for days and then woke up on a cloud.

Woe is me was correct. From that day forward, my cravings for alcohol quickly transitioned into a physical *need* for alcohol. The process accelerated. It felt, tasted, smelled, and looked so good—always.

Chapter 9

Back Home and Principaling

"Home is the nicest word there is."

—Laura Ingalls Wilder

After seventeen years of teaching and after completing a second master's degree in K-12 educational administration, I began applying for principal jobs. I ended up landing my dream job: assistant principal at Webster City High School. After a twelve-year hiatus, Alesha and I would take our children back to Webster City, where we both grew up.

Alesha and I had moved our kids around to various Iowa towns, but Webster City still felt like home, and we were jubilant knowing that our kids would attend the same schools we did, play ball in the same parks, and generally grow up around the same families, just a generation removed. The summer before I began my first year at Webster City High School, I remember going for a small walk. The grass seemed greener and the summer air struck me as unusually pleasant and familiar. *We were home.*

I was elated to be home. I had arrived, and I was so proud of myself. I was ready to help lead a high school, one that had been so good to me in my youth. Many friends living in Webster City received us with open arms. It was the perfect zenith of my career and a high point in our marriage.

It didn't take long for disillusionment to set in. To any educator aspiring to become a building principal in your hometown: Proceed with extreme caution, especially if certain teachers still working there were *your* teachers. Working with my old teachers was a blessing, but the curse comes from the guilt and self-doubt that occurred as I acted outside of what they needed me to be. Our philosophies and perspectives often differed, and it's not fun letting down the people who helped mold you in your formative years. Imagine letting down your parents—smarts a bit, right? Now imagine letting several of them down daily. This is sometimes what it feels like principaling your old school.

High school administration is an interesting career. I taught high school and college classes for seventeen years, so I felt I was well prepared for the task, and in many ways, I was. The students were rarely the problem; I typically always found a way to work with the kids in my class. I can only recall two times when a student's behavior warranted removal from my class.

After I began my new job, I found a student sitting outside of my office, which typically meant he had been kicked out of class. After speaking with him, I conveyed to him that I needed to get the teacher's side of the story. When I spoke to the teacher, he heaved a huge sigh and said, "He wasn't focusing."

You, uh . . . you removed a child from his learning environment because he wasn't focusing?

That's when I knew I might be in trouble with this role, because here's what I know for sure about high school students. They want:

- You to be genuinely engaged in what you're teaching.
- To feel your energy and passion for the subject.
- To know you care about them as people, not just students.
- To feel seen, heard, and important.
- A relationship with you—even when they act like they don't. (In fact, the ones who seem to deserve it least often need it the most. This is true in many areas of life.)

"Behavior" students usually develop a series of challenging defenses and maladaptive actions. Effective educators need to see these behavior barriers as an interesting challenge and be prepared to connect with them by almost any means necessary. In short, you need thick skin and tunnel vision. If you're not juggling these things as a high school teacher, you're going to have classroom management issues that no principal in the world can solve for you.

Some reading this may be saying, "Well, back in my day, kids were disciplined harshly and they learned from consequences." I grew up in that time too, and it may have been better—I haven't really decided. However, if you spend any time in a high school today, you'll quickly see our paradigm has changed. Also, it can be very counterproductive to impose consequences on certain students, particularly those who come from abuse, homelessness, unconscionable loss, absent parents—the list sadly goes on and on.

How do you punish students whose whole existence has been a punishment of its own? Further, does it really make sense to do so?

According to behavioral psychology, if you punish misbehavior enough, the kids who acted out the most should end up behaving the best—because you've essentially trained the misbehavior away. Yet somehow, it rarely works that neatly.

Actually, the sad fact is that so many kids are so emotionally broken. I always felt it was our job as educators to help kids put themselves back together. During psychological studies, if a rat is shocked enough with negative consequences, eventually they simply sit there without responding at all.

They become seemingly numb to punishing conditioned responses, no matter how severe.

I faced so many headaches and conflicts involving parents, students, teachers, district employees, coaches, and players, and they always seemed to make their way to my desk—problems that required me to flip a coin between either a bad solution or a *worse* solution.

Leadership also requires a certain degree of authority. Without it, leaders end up becoming vulnerable and ineffective when attempting to build consensus and make decisions. It's a top concern in educational administration, and many principals I know experience unnecessary and excessive stress and anxiety when their supervisors abandon one of the most basic tenets of leadership: Hire good people and trust them.

Leadership in our district seemed to waver and drift, as if rudderless. I served under three different principals, each with their own unique style. Educational programming and building management in our district lacked definitive anchors. One minute the way we did business at the high school was fine, the next, it was either too punitive, too lax, or worse, unprincipled, not grounded in any sort of virtuous purpose. I felt dizzy many days (not alcohol-related).

Denny Bahr, a retired superintendent, would substitute teach for us from time to time. He was the superintendent when I was a student at Webster City Schools. He observed my frustration without a solid, systematic way of how we intended to handle the day-to-day challenges of the school day. I was often flustered. He once commented, "You know, you can only bend and wield your values so much before you break."

These words proved to be extremely prophetic. I tend to be an extremely conscientious person, constantly reflect on myself, and do well only when a task or mission is clear and when I am made aware of what needs to be done. When this clarity was absent, I struggled, and the struggle seemed constant the more I served as assistant principal.

There is a condition that many educators experience as they toil through the struggles of teaching during the tough times: empathy fatigue. Helping kids through their unmanageable struggles can weigh on you. As assistant principal, I dealt almost primarily with these cases. As good as you try to be for the students, it wears you down and brings about sorrow. If not managed, it can eat you up inside.

I think teaching is the most important job in the world. Developing new neurological connections is a feeling of accomplishment like no other, but it's damn hard work. When I was in the classroom, I used to have conversations with friends in the corporate world who would say, "I have a big presentation coming up!"

I'd ask, "How many times will you give it?"

"Like, three times this week!"

I would counter with a laugh, "Well, I give seven presentations over five different subjects every day to a hostile audience and make about half as much as you. I would gladly trade you."

They'd respond, "But you get summers and weekends off, and holidays!"

Let me stop you there. Just about every teacher I know, especially early in their careers, will work a second job during the summer, and the work will also extend into their time off. Don't even get me started with the prep time it takes after hours to generate quality lessons. It's stressful and tedious, and at times, it feels like you're not really making a difference. It's a business of delayed gratification.

When I worked at my dad's tire store I could mount, balance, and install four new tires, and there they were—visible, right in front of me. With teaching, you only truly know if you've done the job right when a student returns to you at school to say thank you. It's hard, wonderful work, and it's very much an art. Most of the good teachers I know want to be supported by administration and be left alone to make the magic happen in their classrooms.

I began teaching in 2002, and at that point, education hadn't really changed all that much from when I was a high school student. In the decades that followed, massive changes in pedagogy, intertwined with technology, spun teaching into a new age. Along with this came a new wave of professional development programs, companies, and academic initiatives from experts wedging themselves into schools to teach teachers how to teach. Today, teachers not only need to teach quality lessons (lessons they plan themselves), they must meet as professional learning communities (PLC), work within a multi-tiered system of support (MTSS), and generate a guaranteed and viable curriculum based on priority standards. We pull the best teachers out of the classroom to form a teacher leadership community to better teach the teachers how to teach (TLC). Teachers must create socio-emotional learning lessons (SEL) to teach students social skills and emotion management. Advisors from companies (who make billions of dollars per year) carve out dozens of days to teach teachers how to teach.

You know, because teachers don't know how to teach, and must learn a million stupid acronyms on top of that. All levity aside, this new education consulting industry has taken over teacher professional development and the programs and services they provide is often suspect.

The dynamics of parental involvement (or lack thereof) seemed to shift as well. The paradigm I was accustomed to involved the student being in one corner and the parents, teachers, and administrators in the other, working together to provide the best education we could for the child. If the student was having behavioral issues, adult collaboration would ensue. Every year I was in education, it seemed like the parents got further and further away from the educators' corner to join the child, especially with regard to behavior. Without parental support holding kids accountable, it's next to impossible to help students achieve their best school experience.

On the administrative side, you steer the ship with all of these things on board. However, I didn't agree with taking so much of our teachers' time to work with advisors that claim to have a better way of doing things. I believed in trusting and being inspired by our best teachers, growing the younger and developing teachers and showing the ones who didn't want to inspire kids the door. Principals are now crowned "instructional leaders," which is fine, but to me, Leadership 101 involves hiring good teachers and trusting them, giving them what they need, inspiring them, and watching them flourish—not making them jump through hoops, requiring them to listen to "experts" who had never taught in a classroom or who weren't very good if they did.

Many of my teachers were experts, and we should've listened to them and given them money to develop professionally, rather than listening to some middleman market making a fortune off of the presumption that teachers don't know how to teach.

I get the research, and I understand through data analysis, test scores improve if we run our schools a certain way or teach in a certain manner. Karl Marx mathematically demonstrated that industrial capitalism was internally flawed, irrational, and contained the seeds of its own destruction. Fanciful and elaborate explanations as to why capitalism possessed its own seeds of destruction. The top economies in today's world? Still capitalistic or at least profit-driven.

Why? Because it works. We can roll out, invent, reinvent, and innovate within the instructional frameworks, support systems, and data-driven methods of running a school, but when it prevents teachers from truly connecting with one another organically, having time to reflect, recharge, and calibrate their own craft, while bogging them down with busywork for the sake of achieving some utopian end of moving decimals on a standardized test, we miss the mark. Teaching, *real* heartfelt, nurturing teaching, is the key variable here, and quality teachers know how to facilitate and deliver it. They don't need drudgery.

So, should we expose teachers to the research and suggest improvement where it may be necessary? *Absolutely*. But much of what we do as instructional leaders at the administrative level tends to cramp teacher energy and compromise their efficacy and beliefs. *We must do better*.

I had more good days than bad days my first few years in high school administration. I would often daydream about a different line of work—perhaps a pivot out of education, but fear of the unknown and uncertainty, combined with my financial obligations to my family, kept me at my desk. However, during and after the COVID-19 turmoil, things seemed to change. If I felt uncertainty about my job at first, it transitioned into loathing after COVID-19.

Most education professionals during the pandemic will tell you our educational system was woefully unprepared to serve students, and it revealed our antiquated educational practices in serving students who have certainly grown up in a different time than previous generations. However, there is a painful question shrouded in mystery here: *Did I come to loathe my principal work because of my descent into alcoholism? Did its mood dysregulation and withdrawal cause my negative attitude toward the profession? Or was this work simply not for me?* This is a quandary that I frequently grapple with and I will probably never know for sure.

I know one thing: I *do* feel that being tasked to help lead a high school while serving the needs of students (whom we were already failing through a pandemic) created fertile soil for my alcoholism to solidify its roots.

Chapter 10

Full Blown

"How can I blame the wind for the mess it made if it
was me who opened the window?"

—Anonymous

*I'm in Cancún, Mexico! Life doesn't get better
than this!* Arriba, *baby!*

During spring break 2022, I was a
full-blown alcoholic, hiding it like a boss (yeah,
right).

In March of that year, Alesha's sister, Amy,
pitched the idea for her family, ours, Alesha's
brother Hank's family, and plenty of friends to
get away to an all-inclusive resort right on the
ocean. Needless to say, I drank and drank and
drank, but *everyone* was imbibing. My drink
ratio compared to the others was probably
three to one, but who was counting? It was
gorgeous there, with eloquent pools with
fountains and swim-up bars, and opportunities
for endless fun: ziplining, four-wheelers
through the jungle, fine dining with bottles of
wine at night, and an awesome ABBA tribute
concert.

After drinking all day, the crew headed to
the concert and secured a couple tables near

the stage. Amy's twin college-age sons, Gavin and Madox, were near the runway to the stage, trying to get a few of the dance moves down. They were getting the moves all wrong—it just wasn't their generation's dancing. They caught my eye just as I secured my millionth Long Island iced tea for the day and fell into my chair next to Boston and Tessi.

I stood up immediately, despite the fact that I'd just sat down.

"Where are you going?" Alesha asked, but I ignored her.

I made my way through the crowd and said, "Okay, boys, this is how you do it." I went into perfectly timed leg sways with a John Travolta hand wave. Though I was dancing and teaching brilliantly (or so my impaired memory tells me), they just weren't getting it. Something came over me as the band began singing "Dancing Queen."

I said, "Screw it, let's go!" and led a gaggle of young scholars down the runway, clapping my hands. I leapt onto the stage, fully expecting security to escort me out. They were too late, and the beautiful lady ABBA impersonators cleared the way. I dove right into my disco dancing in front of thousands of vacationers and Alesha's entire family. Everyone went crazy, laughing and cheering me on, and it was so much damn fun!

After I got off the stage, people swarmed me, seemingly starstruck by my rendition, my fifteen minutes of fame, combined with drunken bliss. Gavin and Madox were laughing so hard, they were crying. Alesha was rolling her eyes and smiling—she had seen such shenanigans before. During college Halloweens, I had become something of a bad disco dancer while dressing up Saturday Night Fever-style.

What all those people didn't see was the next morning: me running to the toilet and throwing up first thing in the morning, which had become routine. Me, shaking like a leaf at breakfast because I physically needed a drink. I had to keep my hands under my thighs so people wouldn't see. When Alesha went to the bathroom, I rushed to the bar and made a young waiter make me a screwdriver. He poured a generous shot, but I said, "More vodka." The drink ended up with about eighty percent vodka. I gave him a few bucks and rushed back to the table where Boston and Tessi sat, eating their pancakes. Just as I sat down, Alesha came out of the restroom.

Perfect timing, I thought. *Ahhhh . . . No more shakes.*

There's no exact moment when you cross the threshold into physical addiction. No temperature thermometer, no scan, or blood test magically reveals, "Shit, it's just as suspected. This test shows he has alcoholism! Get the straitjackets!"

I had been playing with fire for decades, and there were definitely times I knew I was well on my way. In some ways, I foolishly believed addiction to alcohol was not something that could not happen to me (*I'm Irish, it's part of my heritage*), or if it did, it really wouldn't be that big of a deal. It was a little bit like the movie *Say Anything,* where John Cusack playing Lloyd speaks about love, relationships, the prospect of heartbreak, and proclaims, "I want to get hurt."

Adulting is fraught with struggle and pain: the bills add up, the kids are sick, you're fighting with her again, work sucks. But a special secret lives in your car, the basement, or in the garage. It becomes your refuge as the sting hits your tastebuds: *You feel a brief nervous shock. Then, a shake of the left hand. Close your eyes. Wait. Then relief, relaxation. Your shoulders drop.*

The year or so prior to the day I was sent home represented a year plus of full-blown alcoholism. I gave my addiction full license to reign, and despite my best efforts, I could not control it. This is difficult to understand unless you've been there. I fought the need as it attempted again and again to enter my work, but one morning, I just gave in. My daily drinking tactics varied. Somedays I would hit up a gas station as early as 6 a.m. to buy vodka. Sometimes they'd follow state law and not sell until 7 a.m., but sometimes the clerk would grin and let it fly.

I hit up different gas stations and liquor stores to spread the risk. On my "best days," I'd have different travel mugs with different concoctions at the ready. I always left them in my car. I *never* brought the drinks into the school—there are standards, after all. A steady go-to was a twenty-four-ounce Mike's Harder Lemonade that I would make even harder by adding vodka to "treat" my mood dysregulation.

When you start giving into it at these late stages, it wants more and more. It knows it has all the power and control. It reads your weaknesses because it is *you*—you're the weakness. It's a terrible mutiny, a full breach, its culprits entrenched deeply in your neurons in control of the entire battleground.

Man, I was good at hiding it (or so I thought—I was drunk most of the time). I'd buy 1.75 liters of vodka, bourbon, or rum at a time, but at that point, I was drinking such high quantities that it was simply a matter of having as high a supply as necessary. Surplus alcohol was then a null set. Really, anything worked toward the end. Vodka was cheapest and easier to hide on my breath, so that became my go-to. Plus, it mixed with everything: cranberry juice, orange juice, Red Bull, water. By the end, it didn't really matter—I drank vodka straight.

The thing is, bottles can be really hard to hide, especially big ones. They clink and clank, and they break. Spillage was never an issue as I drank every last drop, but it was nonetheless a bloody nuisance. The plastic containers were much easier to enshroud and discard, and they were recyclable, too! So I bought those whenever possible, though once the big can bin bag in the garage had more than two or three big booze bottles, it raised Alesha's eyebrow, so I kept an eye on that. *Sorry, planet Earth, my clandestine drinking problem takes precedence.*

I hid containers in all of my vehicles, the basement, the garage, and in a few other nooks. The likelihood of being discovered dictated their disguises. I could hide a handle or two of vodka under the back seat of my truck because I rarely drove it, and Alesha never did. In my basement (where suspicions began to arise), I hid Listerine bottles of vodka mixed with green food coloring. Lucky for me, rum and whiskey are pretty much the same color as regular Listerine. I thought I was so smart and novel.

Another story sticks out in my mind. In September 2021, I was getting ready for a huge party at my house. Other than the Iowa State Fair, the annual Iowa/Iowa State football game ranks right up there with what we Iowans consider an international event. I woke up at 6 a.m., poured a large Red Bull/vodka and smoked a whole mess of ribs, chicken wings, and pork loin for barbeque pork sandwiches. Alesha made her famous cheesy potatoes. We turned on ESPN Game Day on all the TVs in the house.

It was going to be a Saturday to remember, and I was in my element. We planned to have about thirty people over. Hutch and his wife, Randi, were coming over, and so were Heather and Justin (Heather was the one who suggested I ask Alesha out years ago).

At this point in my drinking, I made strong drinks in advance so happy, funny Pat would be in full effect by the time company arrived. I'd done it a thousand times: pregaming, getting ready to kick back with friends, and watching some pigskin. Kickoff was set for 2:30 p.m., which was the perfect drunken cycle time: drink hard in the morning, switch to beer during the game, then once game's over by 6:30, the evening would be my oyster to drink whatever the hell I wanted.

As I smoked the meat and set up tables and chairs, put away tumblers of my wonderful elixir, I'd cracked open a new handle of vodka, and it would more than supply me for my daily activities. By the time people started to arrive, I was hugging and poking fun at the Iowa fans, and away we went as kickoff approached.

Into the second quarter (after I'd slammed a couple beers) Hutch said, "Hey Pat, how 'bout a vodka?"

Hell, yes! I can switch back to vodka mixers!

I poured both Hutch and myself a stiff one and noticed the handle of vodka was all but gone.

Okay, someone helped themselves and made a drink of their own, right?

I looked around and realized there were plenty of other open bottles of vodka. *I had drunk an entire 1.75 liter of vodka in just under nine hours.*

Well, I'll bust another one out! By the end of the game, I was staggering around and beyond impaired.

People were saying things like, "Gosh, Pat, you okay?" I felt embarrassed, used the ISU loss as an excuse to be mad, and slinked down to the basement. People thought something was wrong, and Heather came down to console me, but I could hardly put words together to manufacture some sort of emotional toil that I could pretend to be going through.

Heather left and I passed out on the couch in the basement. Alesha showed everyone out after the game—post-game activities were cancelled. Alesha was quietly upset, but I shrugged it off as her eccentric husband who sometimes drinks too much.

The fun times dwindled as my tolerance grew as the addiction demanded. All jovial social highs got choked out by my need for abysmal quantities of alcohol. This sort of drinking slowly became the norm. No fun buzz or a little tipsy. Full bore to impairment and passing out instead. *What fun!*

Occasionally, I would misstep. Alesha would find a bottle of Listerine and throw a look of disgust my way. It was always best to transfer and redirect any alcoholic drinking suspicions toward a prosocial event: "It was from the tailgate!"

About eight months before the hospital, I started vomiting every morning and often throughout the day. I could usually make it to three or so hours of sleep before I needed to wake up and have a few drinks to get back to sleep.

I knew it had me, but I also knew that it ultimately meant I would have to stop. The thought of stopping made my blood run cold.

Once or twice, I tried to confide in others, but when I was about to say that my problem was alcohol, I shifted the conversation to something else or burst into tears, dismissing the whole thing as a moment of sadness.

Over Christmas break in 2022, I was in the basement, half picking up, half cleaning, and 100 percent mixing vodka drinks. It was a splendid no-work day whereby I could sneak ice from the kitchen down to my bar and make cocktails all day. The ice hit the glass that morning around 4:30 a.m. By early evening, I had killed an entire 1.75 handle and was working on a smaller bottle. My friend, Erik, stopped over and joined me in the basement. He stirred a drink as we chatted and caught up. I was watching *Battle of the Bulge* from the 1960s, but Erik was unimpressed with its special features. Before long, my eyes began to well, and I knew that he knew I'd been drinking all day. It was nothing new to either of us. We often went on benders together, drinking early in the morning and late into the night.

Something in my mind slowly tried to sneak a message past the alcohol guards, then finally got through: *You cannot keep doing this. Erik's here. Tell him you need help!*

In our thirty years of friendship, it was only the second time I had cried in front of him.

"What the hell, man? What's wrong?" Erik stared at me through a longish salt-and-pepper beard, wrinkles collapsing around his dark eyes.

The Black Dog, who was dozing in a stupor, awoke and interjected just in the nick of time. "Make something up! You *will not* speak of this so-called problem you think you have!"

So I talked about how Alesha and I were having some problems, work sucks, the kids were expensive—everything but the real problem. He hugged me and said that he was there and always would be.

Then something else happened right after Christmas break that shook me to my toes: a memory of a promising pupil I once taught.

I loved teaching psychology. It was completely new content to the students at the high school level, and most of the time, I could gain the kids' interest.

Justin was one of the brightest students I'd ever taught. He was a tough street kid with blond hair, ripped T-shirts, and dirty jeans. He was tardy in most other classes, swore, and acted completely disrespectful. "Simply incorrigible," his other teachers described him.

But Justin and I clicked. He rarely caused me headaches. He instantly grasped the concepts we covered in psychology and loved the unit on the brain.

I spent as much time as curricular requirements allowed on the neurobiology of addiction. I had suspected that he had done a fair amount of street drugs, because of his swagger and street knowledge. At the end of the unit on the brain, I gave the class an essay test with a prompt: "Explain the brain science we've discussed and how it might impact your life."

Justin eloquently summarized the basic anatomy and physiology of the brain and its functions. He then disclosed:

I am addicted to methamphetamine. I love it even though I know it's ruining my life. I know I'm addicted and will forever long for it. There is no hope. I know it will live in me for the rest of my life. This class has shown me that my synapses have been stripped out and will only release dopamine with my crystal. I wish there was a way out. I know deep, deep down inside that I will forever long for this drug.

I dropped his paper and rested my forehead in my hands. I wanted to help this kid. I could also relate because alcohol was well on its way to doing the same thing to me. I wanted to get sober with this kid, maybe even attend treatment with him. I wanted to save him through myself and my own addiction.

Justin dropped out of school the next day. I never saw him again. I often think about Justin, how promising and smart he was. Under different circumstances, he might've had a completely different life. Justin and his writing summed up where I was at with alcohol and gave me pause. Sadly, my addiction to alcohol simply continued. I fear Justin's addiction flourished as well. If not, I'd love to reconnect with him again. He had so much potential.

You would think that teaching about the brain and addiction would be enough for me to recognize the signs and stop drinking. The opposite occurred: I knew how it worked, so I thought I could control it. The ego, the fucking ego I had: "I'm above addiction because I know how it operates."

Let's see how this works out for us, Pat.

But I'd never gotten an OWI, I went to work at a good job, I was a good dad to my kids. *I just drink too much sometimes.* All of us "high-functioning" alcoholics have it all together. Until one day or one event comes around, and we don't. Research shows that we all have a trigger point whereby our tolerance becomes so high that it triggers a physical addiction. You cross the Rubicon and the die is cast. Every breath, every thought centers around having enough alcohol in your system and you plot to ensure it always stays that way.

I was trapped.

I would stare at myself in the mirror, disappointed that the person staring back both couldn't or wouldn't do something to stop. I remember thinking alcohol would either kill me soon or I'd have to give it up, but the holder of the keys in my brain was *not* going to give it up, so from time to time, I would daydream about how much people might miss me at my funeral. The alcoholism was okay with me dying, so long as we drank all the way to the grave.

It hurt most at three in the morning, both emotionally and physically. What little restraint and defenses against alcohol I still seemed to possess weakened at night. About eight months or so before Matt sent me home,

I would often wake at that hour, shaking and/or needing to vomit. Luckily, I usually had a bottle of vodka nearby, and if I slugged a few gulps straight from the bottle, I might find sleep again.

One fall evening, I threw off the covers and went to my bar to find a bottle. I turned them all upside down—sometimes I'd find a half-full bottle among them. But dozens of handled bottles of vodka and bourbon were all empty. I upturned them all into my mouth, sucking as many droplets out of the empty bottles that I could. I ambled to the garage, where I kept a bottle hidden under my overalls.

Empty.

I checked my truck and sedan, then tiptoed back inside so as to not wake anyone. I found a bottle of wine in the closet pantry just above the coffee, and luckily, the bottle was missing just a few swallows. I quickly drank that and returned outside with the wine to check one more time for bottles in my vehicles. *I needed more.*

I threw up on the front porch as soon as I got outside. I groaned and sat on the front stoop, next to my vomit, staring at my mess in disgust. I was so disappointed in myself. *How could I have not left any alcohol in the house?*

My gaze fell on Lori and Todd's house. *They had a fridge in their garage. Sometimes they left their side garage door open.*

I crossed the street. The door was open. I entered the garage and made a beeline for the fridge. I found a liter of vodka in the freezer, barely touched. Sweet relief awaited, ensconced in a beautiful chilled vodka bottle. I instantly became giddy with joy and relief. I tucked it into my sweatshirt and scurried back home. I had committed a cardinal alcoholic sin: leaving myself without reserves. *So stupid and greedy,* I scolded myself. *We agreed we would never let this happen again.*

Saturday, December 2 (one week prior to the day Matt drove me home) was like most weekends at that time. I started drinking in the morning, looked outside, and I saw my good buddy Todd in his garage.

"What's up, Toddy?" I greeted him on his driveway as he stood next to his freshly detailed black Chevy truck. We often met up at Todd's to plan whose house or garage where we'd drink and watch football. He'd occasionally have sober days, so he wasn't always up for partying, and sadly, my ability to be sober for a single day seemed long gone.

"You stocked up for tonight?" Todd asked, referring to our necessary pregaming prior to the Iowa vs. Michigan Big Ten Championship football game that night. We weren't in shape for a party, so we hopped in his truck to purchase a couple of cases of beer and, of course, a handle of vodka. We parted ways to get our chores and errands done and agreed to reconvene in the early afternoon. I hid the handle of vodka in the dining room—Alesha wouldn't notice it there. I picked some things up in the garage and raked some leaves around the yard and made my way back inside.

Time for a drink.

My heart leapt into my throat when I realized the vodka was gone.

I found Alesha upstairs in our bedroom, where she sat crying, her legs crossed on our bed.

"What's wrong?" I asked.

She began crying harder, her hair covering her face. "Please stop, Pat. Please!"

"It's the Big Ten Championship game tonight! Did you really think we weren't going to pregame at Todd's?"

"You drink all the time now," she said, tears rolling down her cheeks. Her last words ended in a crescendoed panic. "You need help or something . . . I don't know. I'm worried about you. I don't want you to die!"

"I'm fine, honey." I walked into our room and put my hand on her back. "I promise I'll get back to moderating, but let's just have fun today. How 'bout we go to the Saloon? I'll buy us all pizza and wings and we can watch the game there!" By transitioning to a sports bar setting, I could usually smooth over the fact that I was in terrible trouble and did indeed need help. Somehow, it made the situation more socially acceptable.

Alesha cried some more and tentatively agreed. What else could she do? We cast a spell of codependence on our friends and families, which we had to do for the drinking to continue. I asked for the bottle back and she said no.

I stared at her for a second. "Fine," I said. Later that morning, I went out and bought more. She still has that bottle hidden somewhere, a relic of her last-ditch effort to get me to face my alcoholism. Later, in the aftermath of it all, Alesha asked me a simple question, "Why didn't you tell me? Why didn't you ask me for help?"

An honest question demanded a terrible and simple answer: "Because I knew I'd have to stop." Too much has been said about my suffering and not enough about Alesha's. She had to stand idly by as I played her for a fool while destroying her life.

One night, a week or two before my superintendent drove me home, I took my dog, Sherman, on a short walk. I was drunk, as I had been for thousands of previous evenings, and recently, most days. That night, I had drunk beer, followed by bourbon on the rocks (very sophisticated). It was a cold, clear night and the stars were exceptionally bright. I suddenly recalled a time when I was able to enjoy such a beautiful sight sober.

I felt a surge of anger tear through me. I longed to be able to enjoy life again without alcohol.

I'm not a religious person; I'm somewhat of a lapsed Catholic, but I prayed that night. I prayed to find sobriety and be relieved of my job, which I had come to despise. *"Please Lord, I'm in so much pain. The weight of the drinking and the potential to what it might do to my life has me in agony. I can't seem to stop. Please, God, take this thing away."*

Whichever deity was at work heard my nighttime prayer, but the divine slap it delivered was not exactly what I had in mind.

Chapter 11

Demons and Redemption: Intensive Outpatient Rehab

"It was her habit to build laughter out of inadequate materials."

—John Steinbeck, *The Grapes of Wrath*

Journal entry: January 4, 2024

Hey, "Educator."
Hey, "Leader."
At forty-four years old, you should've known better.
There are a million fucking things you could have done to prevent this.
You know that now, and so does your community, friends, and family. Addiction, disease, your past: Aren't these all just excuses? How many times did you tell your players, students, and your children that you wouldn't accept excuses?
Now, here you are with what, quite simply, might just be an elaborate excuse. This means you're weak, lacking character, virtue, and moral grounding. You're an unprincipled person writing a sob story that no one really cares about—of a young, immature,

uninformed, naive person, one who doesn't
know better and who can be forgiven.

You are none of these things. Maybe you
chose this. Whether it was consciously or
unconsciously, who gives a fuck? Freudian
nonsense. At the end of the day, does it really
matter? You shattered a career you spent
twenty-three years building, and you did so in
several Skittle-colored flavors. What's more,
you did it to the same community that once
embraced and loved you in the aftermath of
your parents' divorce—a community that
brought you home to lead.

You took the one great thing that you've
built in this life and corrupted it while
betraying your home. You brought shame,
dishonor, and disgrace to your family name
and jeopardized your home community.

Disease or not, this is inexcusable. You *are*
inexcusable.

I hated myself.

January and February 2024 were two of
the loneliest months of my life, but in a twist of
irony, I wasn't alone all that often. Alesha was
wary of suicide attempts, so she saw to it that I
received regular visitors. I constantly craved
alcohol, in addition to feeling terrible anxiety
and a nagging cough that wouldn't go away
from bronchitis, another fun alcoholic
symptom. I would sit and map out possibilities
as to what my next moves might be: ideas,

arrows, flow charts, scribbles, trying to create a blueprint of some sort of way forward. The priorities were to stay sober and find a job. I generated different tiers of possibilities:

Tier 1: Somewhat idealistic, best-case scenarios

Tier 2: More realistic, down-to-earth possibilities leading to financial strain, such as a lower-paying, lower-status job with bad benefits, terrible hours and strenuous work

Tier 3: Suicide

The weather didn't help. January and February are dark, cold winter months in Iowa. I spent my time sleeping, not eating (I literally had *no* appetite), and smoking cigarettes (a habit from the Marines that resurfaced). Cigarettes and resentment: I do not recommend the combo. I drank seltzers and ignored my dog, who seemed to have a clear understanding of my desire to somehow wake up from this nightmare. And sugar! Sugar helped knock down the cravings a bit. I would sit and watch winter afternoons grow dark in unlit rooms.

I needed help. I knew I could only white-knuckle my way through this hell for so long. As the snow blew outside, the true storm was brewing inside my head.

How was I going to get through this?

My top priorities were to find effective treatment and obtain employment, whatever that might be. I called the counsel that represents the School Administrators of Iowa (SAI), a quasi-administrator's union that I was a member of. I was dying to discover whether my teaching and administrator license had been suspended. But how do you ask such a thing?

"Hi! Pat Farley here . . . Things are really shitty. Turns out I'm a fired alcoholic deplorable. Thoughts on how I can get a job and keep my credentials?"

They said I probably needed to lawyer up. The SAI lawyer gave me a few recommendations for legal representation and sent me on my merry way. I reached out to one of the lawyers and arranged a consultation. The attorney didn't mince words: She said the Board of Educational Examiners would definitely suspend my license. However, if I paid a $5,000 retainer plus fees, she might be able to arrange a shorter suspension. This, of course, was not welcome news. I had just enough savings for my household to stay afloat for four to six months before I'd start panicking.

Alesha and I found an intensive outpatient treatment program. I could work. My mind was hazy and I was emotionally shattered. But I needed to get into the routine of my next career move, whatever that might be.

My career up to this point had revolved around education, so it made sense to return to an endeavor along these lines, but with my credentials in limbo, I wasn't sure where to aim my efforts. The conversation with the lawyer left me feeling completely beat down. I didn't want to spend valuable money toward a "maybe."

Yes, Iowa Board of Educational Examiners, I'm an alcoholic, I was under the influence at work. Over twenty-three years, I had not had one infraction, but if you want to suspend my license, go ahead. Take my job, my credentials, my livelihood. Make it public while you're at it. Do your worst.

I was out of the fight. I was locked in a different fight now: not taking my next drink. But the silver lining was that I could now dream of what a life without alcohol might look like. My newfound sobriety did indeed begin to take hold. My mind kept running the programs to move toward a drink, though I had somehow disconnected its ability to turn these notions into actions. However, make no mistake: I so, *so* wanted a drink. I could taste it, smell it, I would start shaking and trembling as I fantasized about my long-lost friend, who seemed to whisper, *Come back to me. We can be together again. I'll fix everything. Together, we'll make everything okay. Together, we'll devise a plan whereby you can leave me reasonably. What you're doing isn't going to work.*

I wore the same clothes every day: a grey Champion University of South Dakota sweatshirt and green Puma joggers. After every third wear or so, Alesha would wash them. I threw on whatever was lying around, and once dry, I put my unemployed alcoholic uniform back on.

I was broken, clean through the center of my very being. Sometimes I would cry, then laugh neurotically (think eighteenth century-style madness laughing) at how bad things had gotten. I love the Coen brothers movies, and I truly felt like I was starring in my own Coen brothers movie, with humor in the absurd. Amid laughing at my own demise and plight, I also read every autobiographical piece I could get my hands on authored by those who have battled/are battling addiction.

For years, I had read books about either moderating my alcohol use or the benefits of a sober life. Hundreds of personalities and influencers on social media preach their sobriety stories and offer advice, guidance, and support (for money). I wished so badly I could just take the plunge and do it. Now, after everything, I had the strength, though I knew the strength wouldn't be enough. However, Alcoholics Anonymous (AA) was not an option for me for a whole host of reasons.

Although I was dealing with plenty of anxiety and depression, my body was beginning to feel better and better. I had been hungover, fatigued, and in a constant state of either impairment or withdrawal for years. I was constantly dehydrated.

My first intensive inpatient three-hour session was a day away, and I had no idea what to expect. I welcomed the idea of joining others suffering from addiction and experts to help me through my turmoil. I wanted help. I felt so alone.

On January 11, 2024, at 5 p.m., I began my first session of intensive outpatient treatment for alcohol use disorder. It was located at a small treatment center in Ames, Iowa, not far from Iowa State University. The trip to Ames from Webster City took about forty-five minutes. Pulling into the parking lot and getting out of the car, I felt the snow and ice crunch beneath my feet and felt a sense of assurance: *This need to drink all the time needs treatment. And now, I'm going to get the treatment.*

I walked through the door into a small waiting room with a leather couch with a stainless steel frame, two small end tables, and flyers galore strewn about for Narcotics Anonymous, Alcoholics Anonymous, and Gamblers Anonymous.

A man occupied a chair in the corner. He had clearly passed out, which gave me some relief. *Okay, I'm not drunk and passed out, so they'll at least think I'm doing better than that guy. Pat: 1, Drunken Passed-Out Rando: 0.*

A fit young man, sporting fashionable green tapered dress pants, a fresh haircut, and a quarter-zip hoodie greeted me, and strangely, didn't react to the passed-out, greasy stranger in the corner. He walked me through narrow hallways containing posters designed to scare, motivate, and guilt one to refrain from drinking, gambling, narcotics, and unsafe sex.

Upon entering the scantily decorated small office, I learned that my substance abuse addiction specialist could not have been more than twenty-two years old. He had freshly cut black shiny hair and was a little scruffy. Good-looking kid.

"Hi, I'm Scott," he said. We shook hands and made small talk and I learned that he had just graduated from Iowa State with a bachelor's degree in psychology. I believe he was in the process of obtaining a license to be a certified substance abuse counselor.

Here's the problem: I knew (or at least had some idea) of what was going on in my brain and nervous system. It didn't take me long to realize that though promising and bright, this lad was light years away from being able to help me uncover the mysterious motives that caused me to jump into alcoholism. But I played his game. He fumbled through the system administered on his desktop, running me through a battery of questions to assess my substance use and mental health.

"Yes . . . Yes . . . Yes . . . Gallons of liquor. Yes," I dutifully responded.

After the assessment, young Scott administered a urinalysis test. I instantly tested positive for high levels of benzodiazepines from the hospital.

It dawned on me that the program was largely meant to monitor folks on probation and others who had other compliance obligations to the state. I realized I was now at the basic (at best) addiction treatment level. I wouldn't find the answers, work, and help that I sought here, but I tried anyway.

After the assessment and peeing in the cup, they took me to a classroom with mismatched chairs, a particle-board table and various boxes with random objects ranging from Cheetos advertisements to Christmas decorations. A few others sat on the mismatched chairs, and one man made himself quite comfortable, his leg kicked up on the table. A heavyset man wearing sweats and a New York Yankees hat introduced himself as Marco. He sat right next to me, breathing noisily. He produced a Subway sandwich and began enjoying it, sounding like a dog slurping a meal. He smiled and winked at me, and I giggled to myself.

This whole thing is crazy, I thought. I felt an overwhelming sense that I was in trouble, and I was. Scott entered the room, trying very hard to appear confident and friendly.

Okay . . . Three hours. Let's do some addiction stuff, I thought.

So what did Scott do? He handed us all Sudoku sheets and stated that we had thirty minutes to complete them. *Sudoku!*

After Sudoku "treatment," Scott passed around photocopied packets and we read aloud about the process of relapse. We shared a bit about ourselves. I was as candid as I could make myself be. My fellow group members came from various backgrounds. Most were on probation and either under- or unemployed like me. Marco was friendly and talkative, with a pleasant attitude and a great sense of humor. He said, "I drank to get off crack, then used crack to get off vodka and that cycle didn't seem to work for me very well."

Another man in his twenties, who wore big black Drew Carey glasses and disheveled hair, blamed his psychiatrist for using experimental meds on him, causing his addiction to alcohol. *A terrible plight indeed,* I thought to myself. *Was he going to take any responsibility?*

The meeting clumsily concluded, and everyone bolted for the door except Marco, who lingered to offer to bring me a Subway sandwich with his employee discount if I wanted one. I took him up on the offer. The

176

possibility of a sandwich for the next session was probably the best thing I'd get out of any of these.

Here's what I wanted to hear from Scott: *Alcohol owns you and you love it, but it must die in you. The challenge becomes abandoning a version of yourself that makes you comfortable. When you feel that all-important* want *to change, you begin taking a broken and defiant self and gambling on him. The odds and probabilities are very much against you. It's dark, lonely, and terrifying.*

I went to intensive outpatient treatment hoping I might get answers, or at least get help in leading me toward finding my answers. I came to the scary conclusion that I wouldn't find it there.

The next few sessions delivered more of the same. I really did try to get as much as I could out of these sessions. Marco came through with the Footlongs, and another group member tried to sell me some clean urine during a break, which I declined. I was officially becoming part of the gang, though.

After doodling on my crossword (the topic was world rivers) during one session, we watched a documentary that featured celebrities taking a stand against the stigma of addiction. It was actually pretty good, with Courtney Love and an NBA basketball player all speaking on how addiction is a disease, and how we as a society need to do better to promote an understanding of it.

"What did you take from this? What are the key points?" Scott asked.

There was little response as was often the case; two members of the group had just woken up after napping through the film.

I decided to go first. "While this documentary is inspiring, it does not represent the sociological norm pertaining to addiction in our society," I said.

Marco perked up. "Yeah, those motherfuckers out there have no goddamn clue what we going through. They just a bunch of judgemental goofies."

Hear, hear, Marco.

I paid lip service to the "treatment" for eight sessions. I journaled (I assigned myself my own prompts) and I was amused when Scott concluded that I was well on my way to working toward recovery and that I had successfully completed the program. (Darn, no more discounted Subway from Marco.) Scott also wondered if I was interested in mental health counseling.

By this time, I had made various attempts on my own to find a mental health counselor. I asked my doctor for a referral and called various clinics, but reached dead ends. At best, I'd hear a "maybe in three months we can see you." I had kind of given up and was stoked to learn Scott's team included an in-house mental health therapist, so Scott took me to Miranda's office.

Miranda looked to be in her late twenties with cool pink horned-rimmed glasses. Her demeanor did not match the fun glasses—she told me to sit down and typed my Social Security number into the computer. It turned out she was checking my criminal record. "All I see on your record is a traffic ticket from twenty years ago," she said.

I noticed an orange cat sizing me up in one corner and another pillow near her desk with bones printed on the fabric and a light layer of brown fur. I assumed it was for a dog, so I asked.

"He died. It's been really hard," she murmured.

"Oh, I'm sorry."

"Yeah, we can probably see you in like, six months, but without criminal involvement, you're low priority."

"Okay, thank you for your time," I said, and left.

I called around to several offices and got added to waiting lists. I left messages and received no return phone calls.

I was on my own.

The data on successful recovery from alcohol use disorder is not clear because there are simply too many variables. My best approximation after researching data is that roughly eighty-five percent of those who seek treatment for alcohol use disorder will relapse less than a year after seeking treatment. Worse, only ten percent of those seeking treatment are successful in finding it. The intensive outpatient treatment had good intentions, but like so many facets of mental and medical care in the U.S., they lack resources. When you have a problem with alcohol and want help, you have very few treatment choices unless you pay out of pocket. Moreover, if you do pony up the dough, many of the inpatient rehabs focus on philosophical/religious virtues (we are unprincipled, after all), low-quality group and individual therapy efforts, and an overall incomplete understanding of addiction.

One quiet Saturday morning, I was trying to save us a few bucks by working on Alesha's car myself instead of taking it into a shop. I'd jacked it up all the way around so I could rotate the tires, change the oil, and flush the radiator. I was using two-by-fours and some careful balancing to get the fit right with the jacks.

I crawled out from beneath the car, and within seconds—maybe ten—one of the boards snapped. The jack collapsed. I hadn't put the tire on yet. The wheel assembly came crashing down like an angry exhale from fate. If I'd still been under there, that would've been it. No drama. No do-over.

I stared at the car, stunned. Didn't rush to fix it. Didn't yell or curse. Just sat with it, letting the silence do its damage.

My kids . . . They almost didn't have a dad. Alesha . . . She almost lost her husband.

My friends (the few still standing by me) would've wondered. Many would probably have assumed I'd just given up, taken my own life. That would've been the easier narrative.

I don't recommend it, but a near-death experience has a way of clarifying where you stand when it comes to the will to keep living. It's a brutal kind of litmus test, one you don't seek, but if it finds you, it answers questions you didn't even know you'd asked. But something in that moment rewired me. That close call didn't just shake my bones—it shook loose something deeper. I took inventory of my pain, my people, my purpose, and I made a decision.

From that day forward, I stopped flirting with the idea of leaving the world by my own hand. I never told Alesha about my near escape. Once she reads this, she'll likely put the hammer down on me working on our own cars.

Sorry, Cakes!

I didn't do AA.

I have nothing but respect for Alcoholics Anonymous and its mission, though its path to recovery never seemed to align with the approach I began to hypothesize and ponder. I am a proud member of the American Legion Post 907. I love the outreach and charity work, especially in caring for veterans. I often worked with the post commander, a man named Richard Stroner, coordinating Veterans Day and Memorial Day assemblies when I was a principal.

However, during monthly meetings, we start with a mission statement/oath proclaiming an adherence to a host of ultra-patriotic claims that I could not get behind. While I am a Marine and proud American, I also believe democracy depends on discourse and blended views. I'm aware of the historical mistakes Americans have made, and oftentimes, blind patriotism furthers those mistakes. My understanding of the world and interpretation of its lessons generated a few philosophical differences in a strict adherence to the Legion's foundation, though I still believe in their work. This experience encapsulates my views of AA as well.

From a faith and spirituality perspective, I do not at all align with AA's sense of a higher power. The phrase "powerless against alcohol," while I can relate, I do not believe it representative of the recovery mindset I've sought to develop. I also don't want anonymity. I want to sing from the hills that this is a strange and nasty disease like many, many other diseases. We need help and support, not superstitious scorn. Alcoholism carries a stigma, and anonymity is appealing. I want to fight this stigma, and I want to join or lead others in this charge.

I know AA helps many who struggle with alcohol. Years ago, when my drinking was becoming more and more difficult to handle, I considered showing up to an AA meeting and nipping it in the bud with a proclamation of being an alcoholic. In those early days of sobriety, when I truly needed something to assist me in the early stages of battle, I intuitively knew AA would not be it. That notion remains today. Addiction is physiological, progressive, and multi-faceted. Biology is psychology to a large degree, and my plan of attack began with this understanding. AA had little to offer in this realm.

Maybe I should have thrown some money toward a higher-caliber treatment option, but by the time I got to treatment, I was over a month sober. The first month had me hanging by my fingernails wanting a drink, but I survived.

To beat addiction, you must first achieve sobriety. Sobriety means release from the physical grips of alcohol and managing the psychological longing. Recovery is the process of recovering your life and building the life you want. This was the most exciting epiphany once I had a grip on my longing for alcohol. *I can now build a life of my own choosing, no* longer shackled to the agony and cycle of addiction. I emphasize the "I" here because my sobriety and recovery must be my own, and my attack plan must be my own.

Throughout this piece, I've prioritized the WANT as the most important component of sobriety. Why not say *need*? Unfortunately, under addiction's spell, your *need* has been hijacked. You literally need (or at least feel you need) alcohol. The WANT is a flipped switch that creates a motivating action to get sober. It's a battery bringing new energy and force to begin the fight, but it's also temporary. Through life changes, strategies, and techniques to battle the addiction, you create an alternator that returns the charge to the WANT, generating a powerful new force in you. Over time, what started as a WANT to get sober becomes the need to *stay* sober. You have a new life, though as we'll discuss, this mechanism needs constant maintenance.

WANT creates a powerful urge. You'll know it when you feel it. As alcoholics, we have all tried to stop, moderate, resist temporarily, break from drinking, etc. *WANT is different*.

As I walked out of the clinic where I "successfully" accomplished intensive outpatient treatment and into the darkened snowy parking lot, I had a loose grip on sobriety, but not recovery. I was definitely part of the problem with this treatment. I can be a loudmouth and a know-it-all, with an enormous ego, and already had it in my head that Scott's treatment wouldn't work.

What should I do next?

My mind raced. I had a basic familiarity with the different psychological perspectives and ideas after teaching at the high school and college level: Wundt, James, Freud, Jung, Thorndike, Watson, Skinner, Pavlov, Maslow, Piaget, etc. Other than trivially applying concepts here and there to my own life, I had never truly dug in and applied them to myself. I also loved reading Aristotle, Plato, Nietzsche, and Sartre. *Why couldn't I take these ideas, synthesize them, and apply them to my situation?*

Perhaps now that I had a leash on my cravings and urges, I could begin to reason my way out of these woods. I felt a bit isolated and disappointed that I was unable to find resources that might lead me to an alcohol-free life. But I was reinvigorated by my own ideas of how my own therapeutic approach would begin by recognizing my unconscious motivations, bringing repressed thoughts into awareness, and embracing the hidden parts of myself instead of denying them.

I was going to have to do this by myself.

Chapter 12

Confrontation: What the Mirror Doesn't Show

"Reality cannot be ignored, except at a price; the longer ignorance persists, the higher and more terrible becomes the price that must be paid."

—Aldous Huxley

It's really strange that a movie that no one seemed excited about kick-started my efforts to tackle myself psychologically. By late January, I was approaching two months sober. I felt I had blown through something like the stages of grief in record time. The stages were not linear, nor had I achieved them in the same manner as anyone else.

But a tiny bud of excitement began to grow: I was dreaming of a new life. I had long known that my addiction grew within me; I could explain the "why" medically and psychologically. But between psychic reality and emotional discord, I knew a reservoir of ugliness fueled my addiction. I knew I had to get at it, though powerful defense mechanisms guarded it.

Breaching them would require creativity and painful deliberation. I couldn't help comparing it to the beginning of the movie *The*

Exorcist when Father Maron finds a figure of the demon he has battled throughout his career. Knowing he must battle the demon again, he says good-bye to the chief archeologist, saying, "There is something I must do."

The willpower of *wanting to be free* gave way to creating a rough vision of where I thought I might like my life to go. The Black Dog was kenneled, though it stared at me with warm, friendly eyes and whimpered to come out and play. I knew I needed to continue to listen to myself to keep him kenneled. The voice that came alive and successfully countered the Black Dog the day Matt dropped me off had grown and gained influence now. It would drop hints here and there as to what I needed to do. I was starting to believe that we have the ability to know what we need to do to heal ourselves.

Though Sigmund Freud, the Austrian neurologist and father of psychoanalysis, had become somewhat discredited in modern psychology, I believed I needed to walk a path toward him. I can't explain it, but I felt unconscious things were at work with my alcohol addiction, and it made sense for me to gravitate toward his work to dig into my own psyche. Anyone working in any field of psychology would more than likely cite Freud as the most polarizing figure in the history of the field. However, if he were not such an outside-the-box thinker and if he were not correct about so many of the things he theorized, we would not be here in this discussion. There are thousands of scientists who were wrong that we say absolutely nothing about. Freud's work is so vast, and his theories have so deeply impacted our society, that the fragments now considered disproven seem to float on the surface.

In a strange twist of irony, the movie, *Freud's Last Session,* had been advertised in commercials and I wanted to go. Alesha, Chelsey, Boston, and Tessi did not share my enthusiasm, so I had no problem going alone. It was January 24, 2024, a few days after my last intensive outpatient treatment. As snow swirled around the highway, a relentless flurry of white cut through the black sky. My tires ground against icy pavement, my wipers struggled to clear the windshield, and visibility shrank with every gust of wind. I ruefully thought about how it mirrored the battle unfolding within me. The hour-long drive to Des Moines was a quiet act of determination. The snow blanketed the roads as a hush, as if nature itself understood something I didn't.

For decades, I'd taught young minds about Freud, Jung, Adler, Erickson's stages, and the tangled web of the unconscious. Sigmund Freud's work on the unconscious suggests that unexamined desires, suppressed traumas, and unresolved childhood conflicts manifest in our behavior. Freud's theory of parapraxis (slips of the tongue) reveals the hidden mind's efforts to surface past wounds. Healing occurs only when someone brings these unconscious forces into conscious awareness through introspection or therapy.

I understood repression, defense mechanisms, the ways the mind twisted itself to avoid pain. But now, none of it was theoretical. None of it was academic. It was personal. I'd spent seven weeks of wrestling with the beast of addiction. How can I find hope in the most shameful part of me?

When I arrived at the theater, I shook snow from my coat and stepped into the dim, warm hush of the auditorium. The scent of buttered popcorn mixed with old carpet was a strangely comforting reminder of normalcy and of when Alesha and I had worked together at a theater.

I felt as though the film was speaking to me directly, and ironically, not only did I sit alone, I was literally the only one there. Freud's theories echoed in my mind, not as distant intellectual musings, but as keys to unlocking something deeper within me. Perhaps my addiction was not just a habit, not just mere vice, it was the shadow of unexpressed emotions clawing for release. It was psychological warfare, paying out deep in the unconscious, hidden beneath layers of repressed urges, buried pain, and unresolved conflicts. As I stepped back into the cold, a realization settled in: *I don't need a group. I don't need meetings. I'll treat myself.*

The drive home was slow, methodical, the snowfall thicker than before. But something had shifted. As I drove home, I realized I could take the raw tools of psychoanalysis and wield them against the beast that had ruled me for three decades. I'd immerse myself into Freud's work, and with each turn of the page and with each theory I'd dissect, the grip of alcohol would lessen. By the time I pulled into the driveway, the storm had blanketed the streets in silence, unveiling an eerie calm after the chaos. It felt strangely fitting. For the first time in decades, I wasn't drowning. I had begun unraveling the knotted turmoil that lived inside my mind, much of which had been buried.

Once I safely arrived back at home, I threw my coat over the chair, turned on the dim desk lamp, and pulled the first book off my shelf: Freud's *Beyond the Pleasure Principle*. Freud had theorized that human beings are motivated by the pursuit of pleasure and the avoidance of pain. Wasn't that the very essence of addiction? The desperate chase for comfort, the numbing of sorrow, the refusal to confront suffering directly? Drinking had been the ultimate manifestation of this principle—drowning pain in bourbon, quieting intrusive thoughts with the warmth of alcohol in my veins.

But then there was the Death Drive, *Thanatos*, the darker, more terrifying counterpart to the pleasure principle. Freud argued that human beings possess a subconscious urge hellbent on self-destruction, a compulsion to repeat harmful behaviors despite knowing their consequences. Why else had I continued drinking when I knew, deep down, it was killing me? I wasn't chasing pleasure anymore. I was fulfilling an unconscious need to spiral, to destroy, to collapse under the weight of my own existence.

But why? The genetic predisposition, the influence of society, the neurological alterations that occurred as a result of years of using alcohol to achieve the release of unearned dopamine: fine, got it. But *why*?

By dawn, books were scattered across my desk, notes scribbled in the margins, pages marked with highlighters and red pens. I understood now—sobriety couldn't just be about avoiding alcohol. I had to confront *myself,* to battle against the forces inside me that had led me down this path in the first place. Freud hadn't just given me theories; I felt as though I had a firm grasp on a way out. For the first time, addiction no longer felt like an unbeatable monster. It felt like a puzzle that I was learning to solve. I would find a weakness in this enemy from within.

After I flooded my mind with Freud's work, I slept like the dead and awoke with my parents' divorce on my mind. I'd kept a diary from age eight onward. I had tucked many of the diaries away in a trunk in the basement but hadn't read them since I stowed them away in my twenties. I retrieved them and dug in. As I flipped through the pages, they blasted me with emotional pain.

One nugget felt like a knife in my stomach: At the beginning of my parents' divorce, I came home from school one afternoon to find an ambulance parked in our driveway. I remember my heart pounding as I rushed inside, the door still ajar, the air oddly still. Two paramedics were in the living room, gently lifting my mother onto a gurney.

A half-empty bottle of vodka sat on the coffee table like a silent witness to everything that had unraveled. As they wheeled her toward the door, she reached out for Sherie and me. Her voice was fragile, raw, final.

"It's time for me to die," she said.

Sherie and I clung to each other, sobbing uncontrollably, suspended in a moment far too big for two children to carry. We didn't understand what was happening, not really. We just knew something sacred had cracked wide open, and we had no map for the terrain we were suddenly navigating.

This memory—this snapshot of chaos and helplessness—is one I hadn't revisited since my ten-year-old self lived it. It stayed buried, quiet, like so many moments in which I didn't have the language to name.

I hadn't seen much of my mom after that. When my parents divorced, my dad whisked me away to start a new life in Des Moines. He quickly remarried—and *boom!*—we had a new life and family. I never contacted my mother, and she didn't call me, and this arrangement went on for months.

On August 29, 1989, my eleventh birthday, I was sitting at the kitchen table eating Cheerios when I heard a knock at our front door. My stepmother, Connie, answered it, and to her surprise, my mom ran in from out of the rain.

"Mom?"

She hugged me as if I were a life preserver floating in the middle of the ocean. I vividly remember the white scrubs she was wearing. *Wasn't she supposed to be at work? Didn't she know I had school today?* I felt like I had done something wrong, because I knew it wasn't the rain that had caused her mascara to run.

"Happy birthday, sweetheart," Mom said, her voice sounding like she was choking. She hugged me again. My mother felt strangely foreign to me at first, but when I peered into her eyes, I felt an overwhelming longing for her. I broke into tears. She began helping me gather my things for school and tried to pack my school lunch in my dad's kitchen, with Connie looking at us like my mother was crazy.

I began weekend visits with my mom shortly thereafter.

I had repressed my relationship with my mother as I tried to move on from the divorce. By the following winter, I felt depressed after visiting her. I would fake sickness and stay home from school. I longed for her constantly. I cried and cried. I attempted suicide by taking ten Tylenol capsules, thinking it would do the trick, but of course, it did nothing.

My sorrow was constant. At eleven years old, I had no idea what to do with it. I just wished so badly that I could return to a time when my family was back together again.

My dog, Sherman, whom you met at the beginning of my story, has terrible separation anxiety. He cries and howls when someone puts him in his kennel. I cannot put him there; it's the one chore in our household I refuse to do. I'm certain it's because of that period in my late childhood.

I was astounded that I had never really reflected or processed this period of my childhood. My journal from those days was filled with despair. I had written in tight scrawls: *I miss my mom. She is so far away. I can't do this stuff without her.*

I sat in my basement office and closed my eyes. At long last, I spoke to this child. I hugged and reached out to him. I said to him, "This should not have happened to us. Through our struggles and pain, we've survived. You are such a strong young man. Our life has had so many highs and lows. Now we're fighting a new battle, and just as you were reconnected with our mother and a better life, we'll also win this fight."

I cried and cried, inundated with sadness and the pain of long-forgotten psychic shocks and trauma. Recalling repressed memories *hurt* to relive. The anguish was so real, as if it were happening all over again in real time. I called my mother and replayed my memories of the day with her. As a parent, I could now relate to what she must have been going through, because Alesha and I had separated temporarily before. I understood the primal, heart-wrenching longing for one's children.

I continued to read Freud's work and soon branched out into other theorists I thought might help me. I felt invigorated as I pored over old college work and ideas my teachers and professors had stimulated through high school and college classes. I had no idea that one day I would use their lessons to examine my own psyche.

I couldn't get enough of Freud's idea of dream interpretation, particularly after examining my dreams during withdrawal. Freud believed dreams were the road to the unconscious—manifestations of suppressed desires, fears, and unresolved trauma.

My nightmares of drowning, of losing control, of the house I grew up in collapsing around me, weren't random. They were *warnings*, messages from my psyche screaming for recognition.

Next to the Oedipus complex (Freud's notion that children have a strange pseudo-sexual relationship with their opposite sex parent), Freud's *Interpretation of Dreams* is the next most controversial. I was having weird dreams. Something just seemed to be going on up there, more than random firings of neurons that created white neural noise.

I dug into an old dog-eared (and, ironically, wine-stained) copy of the book and reoriented myself with Freud's ideas. I kept a dream journal to identify the symbolism and manifest content of my dreams, but I didn't feel like I was doing any of it right. *Sometimes a cigar is just a cigar.*

But one night, about three weeks after my efforts to gain a better understanding of Freudian dreamwork, I had a dream that either through symbolism, or actual neural communication to my body, changed everything. I dreamed I was in Brewer's Creek Valley, where I spent the best years of my childhood playing in the woods. It was golden hour, and the sun was about to set behind gray clouds. Near a raspberry bush, a large pine tree had a very Mario Brothers-like spigot inserted into it with water or some other liquid running out of it. Suddenly, a boy about eleven years old, with curly brown hair wearing a Metallica T-shirt, walked over to the valve and turned the spigot off. The boy turned and gave me a modest smile.

I awoke in a cold sweat.

Weird.

The following day, I felt rested and energetic, with a feeling of ease about the morning, which was unusual. I went to the grocery store to buy some things and passed the beer aisle. I hated the beer aisle because it was a guaranteed trigger. My pulse and blood pressure would elevate and I'd flush, almost tasting the cold suds.

On this particular occasion, I felt none of that. I felt zero physiological response to alcohol being so close and at the ready. I suddenly had no physical desire for alcohol. My physical symptoms seem to have been all but erased, and since that dream, I've been physically free.

I've spent a lot of time trying to analyze the dream. I decided that boy was my eleven-year-old self, the one I began talking to that fateful night after I'd dug into my diary from the divorce.

I often read excerpts from months and years past from my journal as an adult. There were indicators of when my drinking began to worsen and when it became a full-blown problem. For example, many excerpts were incomplete. I simply stopped writing after berating myself. Toward the end, I'd write, "Are we done with this yet?" or, "Is this really what we are now?"

Since my early twenties, I've dealt with terrible knots in my shoulder blades, especially my right scapula. These knots grew and radiated intense pain the more I dug into dreams, recalled my childhood, and read my diaries. I created life event diagrams, trying to connect my moods, emotions, and gauge my happiness through different periods of my life. This work continued for months (and still does today). I deployed everything I could to try to make sense of my past. Before long, my basement looked like Dr. John Nash's office from the movie *A Beautiful Mind*.

In the fractured pages of my journal—where the writing stopped, as if I couldn't bear to face the truth of my addiction—I stepped in and finished the entries myself:

November 13, 2023: *Are we fucking done with this yet?*

February 14, 2024: *Yes, Pat, it is now over. I'm so sorry we did this to us. But it is over now, and we are working on the life that we should've always had. We will build happiness, a sort of real happiness and fulfillment. This doesn't make sense right now, but there will be a day when alcohol is but an afterthought, we won't crave it, we won't need it, and God willing, we won't even want it. This we will do together.*

Here's the deal with dreamwork that I've come to conclude: Even if it's all bullshit, say Freud and the mystics are just dead wrong, and there's no mysterious link to dreams and reality or wish fulfillment, the very process of attempting to derive meaning from them is an action of deep reflection and self-study. They are our dreams after all, very personal and often containing real memories, sensations, and longings that we may have forgotten, perhaps intentionally. Dreams are often very powerful experiences casting situations, emotions, people, and places that live in our brain somewhere. Thus, at worst, it's a worthy exercise to look inward and reflect a creative and original assignment of self-study, perhaps worthy in and of itself.

I brought Carl Jung into the mix. Jung expands on Freud's ideas by introducing archetypes, universal psychological patterns buried within the collective unconscious. It has been said that in early psychology and psychoanalysis, Freud dug the foundation/basement, and Jung built a house on top of it. Jung believed that psychological healing emerges from integration of the shadow self, the darker aspects of one's identity that society and the individual repress. To confront one's shadow is to free oneself from the burdens of self-deception.

I had implemented elements of deep discussions with my shadow self almost daily since I got sober. But like most alcoholics, my ego was huge; it's how we justify and rationalize the deceptions we use to fuel our addiction.

We lie. You'll only be a successful addict as far as your skill in deception takes you. Dysfunctional, huh?

I was selfish. I had a hard time enjoying the good aspects of life if they didn't benefit or highlight me and if they didn't carve a path toward the next drink. My key goal with this work was to reestablish and reconnect empathy and compassion in myself once again, to become more purposeful in my day-to-day interactions. These characteristics had eluded me for some time. I wanted to truly feel what others felt and connect with them. I wanted to feel sadness and tears for somebody else, to shed this selfish cocoon. It wasn't just my parents' divorce baggage that lingered in my unconscious reservoir.

December 11, 2017 was a fairly typical school day at East Marshall High School. I made my way to work and went into Scott's classroom to shoot the breeze with other teacher buddies: Scott (math), Ryan (history), Rob (grounds crew), Jordan (science), Denny

(P.E.), Justin (special education), Christian (government), and Mike (business) for thirty minutes or so before the start of classes.

We'd drink coffee (just coffee) to talk about sports, politics, news, whatever. I was so blessed to have so many guys with whom I could connect. It's kind of rare in education to have a crew like this, especially at a smaller high school. Mike wasn't there yet, which was unusual. We were in the middle of carrying on when Trent (school counselor) burst in and said in an urgent voice, "Ummm, we just got off the phone with Mike's wife and he hasn't been home since last night. Nobody knows where he is."

Later, we were shocked to find out he'd committed suicide.

I was very close to Mike. He was a confidant and influenced all of us. We discovered later that morning that Mike had taken his own life. Mike was in his fifties and seemed to have it all together. The alpha of our group, he was smart with money and quick to give financial and life advice, which often proved to be very wise. He had a great home in Ames, Iowa, with no mortgage, a wonderful family with a beautiful wife and two daughters heading to college. Mike had been a college basketball player and became an accountant. He left accounting to coach and teach business. Mike lifted weights every day and had a fantastic physique. Standing six-foot-five with silver hair, we dubbed him the "Silver Fox." A passionate and gifted teacher, he had meaningful relationships with his students.

The day Mike died, administrators asked if we needed to go home to grieve. I declined because I needed to be there for the kids, many of whom loved Mike as much as I did. I pulled myself together and gave my classes the best pep talk I could. Most of my kids had Mike as a teacher or were currently in one of his classes.

Like with any sad occurrence in my life at that time, I was sad for a while, but then just moved on. I drank heavily alone in my basement to battle the pain of Mike's suicide. I never truly grieved Mike until I got sober. Only then did I begin to feel the weight of what I had buried.

Around this time, Alesha and I also uncovered that our children were being abused at the daycare they attended. For them: therapy. For me: whiskey.

I turned to philosophy to overcome suffering. Friedrich Nietzsche saw suffering as a necessary catalyst for growth. His concept of *amor fati* (love of fate) suggests that individuals must embrace life. This includes hardship as an opportunity to craft their own strength. In his concept of external recurrence, Nietzsche asks: *What if you had to live your life exactly as it is—every joy, every pain, every moment—over and over again, for eternity?*

Nietzsche is serious here. He wants us to play this out, not metaphorically, but literally. Every detail, every breath, every heartbreak, every triumph—repeating in the same sequence, forever. Nietzsche saw this as an assessment to be used to examine one's life. If you could say "yes" to eternal recurrence, you were truly embracing your existence—flaws and all. This was a heavy idea for me, but also empowering. It allowed me to examine ways in which I might live deliberately, to shape a life I'd be proud to repeat. I wrestled with this for some time and continue to do so today.

Can I censor the part of my life that contains my alcohol addiction?

No, but I realized I must use my addiction as a catalyst to transform my life into something that would not have been possible without it. I adopted an attitude that this suffering from my addiction to alcohol is part of my life and that I need to get to a place no matter how far away, whereby I wouldn't desire to change a single thing about it. This seemed so daunting, so untenable. Yet I recalled that some who have battled addiction and recovered have said, "It's the best thing that ever happened to me."

I wanted to be able to say the same.

Nietzsche also suggested willpower is the driving force behind transformation, urging individuals to create meaning beyond societal conventions. This is a big part of my WANT notion. In *Thus Spoke Zarathustra*, Nietzsche introduces the concept of the Übermensch, or developing traits to become our own superman. I wanted sobriety and recovery to be at the center of growing into a man acting on his endless potential.

I recalled a lecture in which my professor discussed Jean-Paul Sartre's view that we're all empty canvases. I imagined myself painting over my drunken life with a strong primer and starting anew. Sartre's brainchild was existentialism, which asserts that human beings are condemned to freedom. We are fully responsible for creating meaning in a world devoid of inherent purpose. Sartre's philosophy is therapeutic because it forces me to own my choices, however painful, and accept that meaning emerges not from external validation but from my personal commitment to my existence. Our existence brings about its own meaning and evolves with every experience. We need only to be aware that this process is ever occuring.

Both Nietzsche and Sartre encourage facing suffering with radical self-honesty and actively construct meaning rather than passively inheriting it. Through my interpretation of their work, I created a bucket list of experiences I wanted to achieve. I was becoming truly excited for the first time since I could remember. Not just "I want to be a billionaire," goals, but truly life-enriching experiences that I hope will complete my life in all the necessary ways. Nietzsche especially shook me in necessary ways. I was sick of feeling sorry for myself, sick of self pity.

I thought, "I'm a Marine, dammit," and although I knew I couldn't grit and white knuckle my way through this, I also realized that self-loathing and living in my own personal misery would no longer be helpful. It was time to be done grieving this thing, done with the "poor me" routine. In recovery, there's a time to stand up; this was becoming mine.

One more: Plato's *Allegory of the Cave* symbolizes the journey from ignorance to enlightenment. I won't go through the whole allegory, but basically, it suggests those trapped in the cave mistake shadows for reality, living under false assumptions. Only by turning toward the light can they see reality for what it truly is.

I would say that seventy percent of my life with alcohol found me in one of these proverbial caves: In my twenties, I spent my time in bars and clubs, surrounded by people I didn't know nor really cared to know. Then, later, I spent my time in garages and basements, chasing the elusive buzz that "made me fun to talk to" or helped me "find commonalities with someone else."

I told myself again and again that as long as I had alcohol, I would continue to keep company with others chained to their seats, identifying with the shadows. Plato's framework applied to my therapeutic healing in that addiction, depression, or self-sabotage would often stem from my distorted perceptions of life. Recognizing false beliefs (e.g., alcohol is fun and people who drink alcohol with me are fun) and replacing these false beliefs with the pursuit of truth has allowed me to work toward breaking free from psychological chains.

By merging psychoanalysis, existentialism, and philosophical wisdom, I attempted to craft a therapeutic approach that would lead me toward healing, self-awareness, and personal belief. I used an arsenal of methods and strategies to get sober and recover, though digging into my subconscious mind and using philosophical concepts to make sense of my suffering became my real change agents:

- **Confront the unconscious (Freud and Jung):** work to uncover repressed emotions and integrate my unconscious self. Find and dig into the unconscious reservoir where the old hurt lives and pulsates. Make sense of my past.
- **Find strength in suffering (Nietzsche and Sartre):** Embrace hardship as fuel for transformation and take radical ownership of existence. I possess the power to do the work that only I can do. Stop the self pity. Stand up!

- **Escape the mental cave (Plato):**To take on the task of challenging distorted, superficial beliefs and pursue authentic self-knowledge. Alienate yourself from that which truly does not matter.
- **Create meaning (Sartre's existential choice):** Recognize that identity and healing are self-determined, requiring active engagement rather than passive resignation. More than just hope and faith. Intentionality. What would my new world look like devoid of alcohol?

One of my biggest breakthroughs came from this deep work. I believe I was living out of alignment with who I truly was for a long time. I was a fairly introverted child, but kind and hyper (lovely combination). I believed people were good. I constantly felt sorry for people and was extremely compassionate. My mother was extremely kind and loving, and I took after her. My father would show glimpses of kindness from time to time, pay lip service to the notion at church on Sundays, then fulfill the notion that *life is going to be harsh, unfair, and cruel. As a father, he believed he should prepare him for it by exposing a boy to such things.*

There's a profound difference between excavating emotional wounds to understand the origins of our behavior and thinking patterns, and using those wounds to justify stagnation or deflect accountability. True introspection isn't about self-pity or assigning blame, it's about locating the roots so we can replant something better.

To seek reason is to ask *why*, not to escape responsibility, but to illuminate it. It's the rigorous process of tracing behavior back to its birthplace so that change isn't just surface level, but cellular. When done with honesty and courage, this kind of reflection empowers transformation rather than enabling inertia.

Excuses, on the other hand, offer comfort without growth. They defend the status quo, often disguising themselves as logic. But the goal (especially in healing, sobriety, and personal evolution) is never justification. It's restoration. It's about becoming more aligned, not more defended.

Growth demands discomfort, accountability, and the humility to say, "I didn't cause all of it, but I sure as hell caused a lot of it. Now, I'm responsible for what I do next."

I've come to believe that you truly cannot heal without deeply walking through your childhood "stuff." During childhood, so much of who we become is hardwired into us (both positive and negative), reinforcing certain behavior and actions. If they are unhealthy, they imbue shame, guilt, self limiting negative beliefs and emotional pains. These things boil and fester and are the chief cause of many of our problems and roots of unhappiness later in life. My work with introspective psychoanalysis and philosophy ended up being an effort to clear old neuro pathways and channels and work toward rewiring them to stop endless patterns of dysfunctional thinking and behavior.

I was plowing through life! The problem is that my engine was overheating and I tried using alcohol as a coolant. Life hardens us, and we gradually become so willing to fit into the crowd, to please people, and to chase success, that if we're not careful, we risk betraying our own nature. We can become so out of alignment that something has to give at some point. I learned to socialize and portray an extroverted persona using alcohol. It turned on switches and allowed me to be a much funnier and livelier version of myself. It made me prosocial (until not), yet was extremely artificial, a counterfeit life.

I also discovered I'd been living in a constant state of feeling of inadequacy as a father. I love my children so much, though there existed a recollection of my childhood despair and the inevitable conclusion that as a father, I would bestow a similar childhood fate upon them. I would just recreate the same chaos that I endured as a child for my children to experience. My biggest fear was that my children would have to face things that I faced. Certain parts of me told me this was unavoidable, but I finally had the wonderful epiphany this was not so. I'm a good father, and the thought of finally living a life without alcohol brought solace that I could be far better at the most important job I'd ever have.

It's easier for me now as a middle-aged man to to look back and seek to return to elements of who I was in childhood. I no longer really need the dog-eat-dog mentality, though it's worth wondering what my life would be like had I not allowed myself to be swept away into an unanchored life that perhaps was never meant for me.

This process is ongoing and will probably be so for the rest of my life, an anchored psychological excavation. It may be easy to read this chapter and see something of a quick fix, it is anything but. My current self-work revolves around the source and processing of the guilt and shame I feel: handling and processing the endless soundtrack in my mind of shame for the actions of my former self, the rumination of things I did while drinking, and chasing ghosts in time travel.

I felt so much guilt and shame about the impact my addiction would have on my children. They had been so looking forward to being at the high school with me, and I robbed them of that opportunity because of my drinking. I was a good father, but would I have been a better one had I not been drinking?

Without a doubt.

I've always had a strong relationship with my children. But like many alcoholics, I told myself that my drinking wasn't really affecting them. *I was still present, right? I hugged them. I loved them. Spent time with them. I went to their games, concerts, and school events. I provided for them and celebrated their milestones.*

But pretending my addiction didn't impact them is delusion. That kind of denial is how alcohol protects itself.

About ten years ago, my dad was staying with us before driving to Chicago for a Cubs game. That evening, as Alesha, Tessi, Boston, Dad, and I sat at the table, Boston, being a typical messy kid, was spilling food as he ate.

I snapped at him, "Put your chin over your plate like I've told you a thousand times!"

He looked up, frustrated and bold. "Oh yeah? Well, maybe I should tell Grandpa that you drink like twenty-four beers."

He was *five.*

I froze. Boston's comment was laced with courage, honesty, and, yeah, some spite. But mostly it was the truth. My son saw me. He knew. And at that moment, I had to ask myself: *Is this okay? Are we actually pretending this is normal?*

And then, like it always did, the Black Dog showed up, that manipulative whisper of addiction. It was still a puppy then, and it offered comfort disguised as reason: *He's just a kid. You're fine. Most dads drink beer. Relax.*

My dad didn't respond. Maybe he didn't hear. Maybe he didn't want to. Maybe that's how it sometimes works with fathers and sons.

Nevertheless, that moment stayed with me. It was a small crack in the wall of self-protection, one of many that would eventually bring it all down.

They knew, one way or another. Over the years, my children saw through the cracks, felt the distance, and carried the weight of loving their dad through the fog.

After having breakfast and opening a few nice gifts on Father's Day after getting sober, I brought Boston and Tessi down to the basement for an apology.

"I'm sorry I let you both down. I'm sorry I can't be a principal at the high school when you guys are old enough. I developed a sickness with alcohol, and it's work that I can no longer do," I said through uncontrollable tears. I continued, almost choking out the words, "Being you guys' dad has been the privilege and honor of my life. You both are going to do great things with your mom and me by your side. I just want you to know I'm sorry."

As I blubbered, Boston tried hard to be stoic and brave. He even gave me a little pep talk. "It's all right, Dad. You're a great dad," he said, not knowing exactly what to say. Tessi started crying with me and gave me a big hug. They seemed okay.

I'll probably never know the true toll of my addiction on my children. I knew I fell short as a father, but my biggest fear and motivation was to prevent my kids from experiencing what I did as a child. I wanted to preserve them from the drinking and anguish. I worried other kids might make fun of them because of me. I worried they might develop this terrible thing through my genetics. Today I speak openly and candidly to them about alcohol use and how it can turn into a disease. I cannot undo the past—all I can do is use my recovery to move forward and be the best father I can be.

Boston and Tessi have always loved me—loyal, unwavering, even during the storm. But now, in recovery, that love feels different. It breathes. It returns with clarity, humor, and gentle exchanges that no longer have to navigate around pain. What was once shaped by shadows is now reshaped in light. Their smiles come easier. And the way I hear them—*truly* hear them—makes it all feel brand new. The bond was never broken. It was just waiting for this moment, when love could stretch fully, freely, in both directions.

As Tessi walked upstairs, I held Boston back for a moment. I said with tears in my eyes, "One day, you'll be a father, and you will fall short, as all parents do. And you will have to bear the pain and anguish and know what it is to pray for forgiveness while apologizing to your son for not being enough."

Breaking down on Father's Day was cathartic for me. It was a turning point.

I thought, *Now I can be the man and father I want to be. Now I can truly live my life for them, Alesha. Now, I can live my life for me.*

At the risk of acting as something of a philosophunculist, studying classical philosophical and psychological concepts, and personally applying them to my life, broadened my life's scope. What essentially began to take hold was an unwavering desire to take this experience and transform it into something that I'd never want to live without. Leaving alcohol behind for me wasn't a staircase, it became a room. A quiet one where I sit with myself without flinching. Where the past doesn't have to be rewritten, just integrated. I didn't heal by becoming someone new, I healed by remembering someone old. Buried underneath bravado, under performance, old pain, under so many masks. The problem was that I forgot which face I started with: my purpose.

What is my purpose? This question has become the greatest ponderance of this work. Not what are my values or principles, or passion, but purpose. In asking this age-old question, I enter an ocean of meaning and experience that needs sifting. It's fulfilling in ways chemical-induced dopamine delivery never was. I find renewed peace. I find hope. And in doing so, the craving, desire, and longing for alcohol has slowly dissipated.

P.S. Since I began this deep work, for the first time in more than twenty-five years, I've ceased having trigger-point knots in my shoulder blades.

Chapter 13

Alcohol and Society

"There are zillions of people who say that alcoholism is a disease, but not many of them believe it."

-Mercedes McCambridge

When Bill Wilson helped create AA in 1935, alcoholism became viewed and theorized to be a somewhat treatable disease. In the last twenty years or so, our understanding of the human brain has truly come out of the Stone Age. Through brain imaging technology and more advanced neurological research, we have a much better understanding of how the human brain functions. (Though in many areas we're still clueless.) Virtually every study to explore the nature of addiction attributes the condition to changes in the brain. Addiction, like much of human behavior, wavers between nature and nurture. So what about nurture in our environment? What about alcohol and society?

I love baseball. I'm a Boston Red Sox fan, but with Wrigley Field a mere hours from my home, I frequently made trips with friends and family to Wrigley Field, especially on the rare occasion when the Red Sox play the Cubs.

Wrigley became one of our favorite places, particularly because it's smack-dab in the middle of a neighborhood in northern Chicago. One minute, you're walking through a residential neighborhood, and then, through the trees, you see that big beautiful sign: *Welcome to Wrigley Field.* Of course, drinking was always a key feature of the fun. A two or three block area around Wrigley Field attracts stores, restaurants, and of course, many, many bars.

Old Style beer was the homegrown Kraeusened Chicago beer. Budweiser has slowly absorbed that market share, though there's still plenty of Old Style to be had. I'd drink as much as I could before the game and smuggle small shooter bottles into the game (booze is expensive inside). Heavy alcohol consumption in this environment is normal and encouraged, and naturally, I thrived there. I always got a kick out of the synonymous Old Style logo entwined with the Cubs' logo, so much so that on one weekend getaway trip to Wrigley with Alesha, I had an Old Style logo embroidered on a onesie for our soon-to-be-born son. *A beer emblem on one of my unborn child's first garments.* I laughed, and Alesha thought it was kind of cute. Beer, hot dogs, and baseball: It was as American as apple pie. The truth is that I sought to normalize and celebrate alcohol use in any way that I was able to.

Alcohol is inescapable. For those of us addicted to it, the messages of its advertisements are like music to our ears. Normalizing is one of the keys for addiction to thrive. Even if it means paying for small beer advertisements on newborn swag, which will work to potentially enlist them in the ranks of alcohol addiction someday. It is difficult to understand how a glass with some liquid in it can have such a remarkable hold on us. *Strange brew indeed.*

Human beings are social creatures. We enter the world as infants and begin learning the demands of human life. Our senses take in smells, noises, tastes, and we feel our parents' nurturing. We take on challenging tasks that are just right for us as we develop from infants into children. Soon we learn that to be loved and successful, you must do *this* or *that*.

My earliest memories involved adults drinking wine and beer, and I assumed it must be really good until I had a taste myself and discovered it was really fucking weird and bubbly and . . . gross. *What was the big deal with this stuff?*

Soon it was the Bud Bowl (Bud Light versus Budweiser bottles and cans of beer playing at halftime), the Budweiser Clydesdales on beautiful mugs we displayed at Christmas, and Old Milwaukee commercials. And who can forget Spuds McKenzie, the delightful original party animal bull terrier who donned Ray-Ban sunglasses and who relaxed poolside with beautiful bikini-wearing women? I definitely wanted to be part of that crowd! And Budman, a longneck-toting superhero with a cape! By the time I was a teenager, I took my rightful place at the table and imbibed. Over time, it became part of a lifestyle, and for some of us, an addiction.

Our founding fathers didn't invent our ideas for our American style of government. Our constitution was largely patched together through compromises and social contract philosophers and theorists from France and England. "Social contract" in government means that we, as citizens, enter into a collective contract with the government: We agree to pay taxes, obey laws, serve in the military if called upon, etc. In return, we obtain infrastructure, protection, services, and can pursue life, liberty, and the pursuit of happiness (John Locke actually said property, but whatever. . .). We believed England violated our rights, so we fought to break away and start anew.

There's a form of social contract with society and alcohol as well:

- You will be expected to illegally drink by age 17.

- Many parental and authority figures will look the other way when drinking after high school, "boys being boys."
- You'll devote at least one weekend night a week to drinking alcohol.
- Typically, the more you drink, the more social rewards you'll receive.
- Thou shalt drink while watching and attending sporting events, and certainly if you take up golf.
- Should you attend a Saturday morning college or professional football game, you will begin drinking almost as soon as your feet touch the grass on the tailgate spot. It's also important that you drink right up until you enter the game and preferably after the game as well.
- If you are truly an adult having fun at any sort of celebration, you will drink.
- You will drink if you're anywhere near a body of water or a beach.
- Should any meat of any kind be placed on a grill or a smoker, thou shalt drink alcohol.
- Hunting (and especially fishing) will involve beer.

Then it begins: You're drinking on weekday nights and all day Saturday and Sunday. Gradually, you sneak in drinks during the workday.

"No, no, no," you say, "you don't really get it, do you? What you're referring to is alcoholism and you're breaching the contract. You don't want alcoholism!"

The Black Dog responds, "Knock it off, loser. Go back to the social contract of acceptable times for impairment and heavy drinking that we have carved out for you."

"I can't. I think I have to stop . . ." *But I can't stop . . . I start throwing up and shaking and stuff when I stop.*

"You idiot! No, there's no stopping! Hundreds of millions of people drink our product without developing whatever problem you seem to think you have. Suck it up and check out this new commercial."

The 80/20 rule is a governing law in business. Twenty percent of pigs provide eighty percent of all pork, twenty percent of this demographic will buy eighty percent of a particular car produced, etc. The alcohol industry knows that roughly twenty percent of its customers will drink eighty percent of its product. Normalizing this consumption for the heavy-drinking customers is the name of the game. Some will trigger an addiction, but that's not their problem. *Stay thirsty, my friends.*

Thus, in order to get sober and build recovery, we have to develop an immunity to alcohol advertising and marketing. Sounds easy, but it's not for us. The beer in the commercial, the cowboy drinking whiskey, the lightly bearded man in a stylish suit holding Grey Goose: it might as well be magnetic.

We all hear about the stigma of addiction, especially alcoholism. The word itself often reverberates negativity: "He's an *alcoholic.* They're *alcoholics.*" The term almost automatically denotes an inferior person. It's an entirely different experience to live with this stigma, a sort of condemnation. When I started my recovery journey, I thought societal perception of addiction to alcohol and other drugs had improved, but it hasn't, and here's why: People who hear of my disorder immediately assume I sleep under a bridge.

To begin your journey of sobriety and recovery, you have to find that all-important *want* and prepare to initiate a whole new way of living. What you don't have to do is explain yourself to a world that either doesn't care, or worse, wants you to drink and judges you harshly for *not* drinking. I went to a few garage gatherings as a newly sober person, convinced I could and should continue to lead my old life minus the alcohol. I didn't make a speech. I didn't announce anything. I just stopped drinking.

But the room noticed. Not because I was loud, but because I wasn't. Because the glass stayed empty. Because the guy who used to be the life of the party was suddenly just . . . *there.* They knew about the dismissal. The fallout. The headlines. So when I showed up sober, it wasn't seen as growth. It was seen as damage control.

"It's not the drink—it's him," someone said. And that stuck. I became a cautionary tale. The guy who couldn't handle it. The one who must've snapped. Sobriety didn't earn respect—it triggered suspicion, like I'd brought something contagious into the room.

No one asked what I was working on. They just watched and I felt the shift. The way people leaned away. The way laughter got quieter when I walked by. The way my silence got interpreted as shame. But I wasn't ashamed. I was just tired of explaining and pretending. Tired of being the version of myself they were comfortable with. So I stayed quiet, because I knew what they didn't: that sometimes the most honest thing you can do is show up different and not explain why.

It is unfathomable to some I've decided never to not drink again. Alesha was talking to a coworker a few months into my recovery and the coworker asked, "When is he going to drink again?"

Alesha said, "Oh he's not. He's working hard at creating a life without alcohol."

"Right, I know," the nitwit replied, "but, like, when is he going to be able to have a beer again?"

Some folks just don't get it, and that's okay. Bear in mind that it's not your job to educate the world as to why you've given up the drink.

However, are you immune to everything? No way. You'll also feel loss, ostracism, alienation, and an all-encompassing feeling of missing out (FOMO). It is these unpleasant feelings that I believe you must pay special attention to. I predict you'll find that in many settings, it is the drink that you're missing, not so much the people, places, or events. By taking them on and digging to their roots lies the beginning of finding peace in your new life. There are things you have done in the past that you truly enjoy; it's just that you just haven't experienced them without alcohol in a long while. So much of recovery is trial and error. Just know that you are going to have to make life changes. You cannot expect your brain to give you constant sober signals while you're still going to bars or on that annual camping trip where the booze flows. Your brain will be confused, and of course, you'll want to drink. Without careful planning and a willingness to modify who you were, you risk relapse.

Prepare to develop thick skin and an indifference to judgment based upon puritanical superstition and a legion of indoctrinated drinkers.

In reality, most people won't care. A lot of the perceived judgment is in our heads and the majority of people out there are light drinkers or perhaps don't drink at all (oh, to be one of those!).

Recovery for me truly started when I realized life is a series of closed chapters: I'll never play organized sports again as I did in high school. I served my contracts in the military and hung up my uniform. My football coaching whistle hangs on a team picture. Drinking, like so many chapters of my life, has closed. Once I accepted this, it allowed me to be excited for a simple life of waking without withdrawals, enjoying a low-stress job, and saying good-bye to financial strain due to buying alcohol. This simple life presents me with peace and a launchpad to build from, to build and connect with a life I truly own and which organically generates real meaning and possibilities of happiness. It's also a symbol of triumph—proof that I've overcome one of the most complex and grueling battles a person can face.

When you choose to quit drinking alcohol, your world will change. Your social circle will shrink and your desire to go certain places will wane, leaving a void you'll find challenging to fill. People will not understand, or if they do, they often possess an incomplete understanding of what you're trying to achieve. After you break away from the physical attachment to alcohol, you create an enormous void, a void you must fill to stay alcohol-free. This is the essence of recovery. You are now faced with swimming against societal currents toward a journey of self-discovery and meaning. You'll be without the best coping mechanism on which you've come to rely. It's scary as hell and emotionally painful at the beginning.

But it's also incredibly exciting. In recovery circles we speak of the "pink cloud" as a metaphor for a euphoric high many of us feel as we begin to feel a brighter future. It's exciting and new because many of us had not had this feeling of optimism in our midst for years, possibly decades. Alcohol had the reins of our optimism, and made sure that its path always led to it. Sadly, this pink cloud is somewhat short-lived. Soon, most transition into a "What now?" conundrum. Here, you stand before a great canyon of possibility that was unavailable to you for so long. The cravings are gone, your head gets clearer, you rarely feel sick, and you begin waking up in the morning feeling physically well, free of battling hangovers all day. Most importantly, you are *present in your life*, no longer borrowing happiness from a tomorrow which has little to give.

Chapter 14

Sobriety Becomes Recovery

"I will continue to fight for the person I was, the
person I've become
and the person I still have yet to be."

—Samira Vivette

Journal Entry: November 9, 2015

*Quitting isn't always quitting—there comes a
time to break it all down;*
*A polished shoe must be stripped down to shine
again another day.*
Success may not be ours to decide or define;
*Uncertainty and despair become optimism and
hope.*
*Failure becomes opportunity—my work is far
from done.*

Throughout my addicted life, my inner
voices, thoughts, and random dreams of a
sober life sometimes surfaced, as evidenced in
this journal entry from ten years ago. I denied I
was an alcoholic for years, though I prophesied
I'd become one as a teen. I had no intention of
quitting alcohol when I wrote this journal
entry, though somehow, my future battle
seemed written in the stars.

We live in a world of quick response, instant social media stimulation, technologically triggered gratification. Once you get into this thing, it doesn't take long to conclude that that is not how recovery is going to work. I estimate I achieved sobriety within days after my last drink on December 8, 2023. Some sobriety work paralleled my transition into recovery, but certainly by March 2024, I had a grip on sobriety and truly began feeling a longing for a life without alcohol. It was no longer a dream or a *maybe*—it was *anchored*. I generated a new lifestyle, a clear mind, and daily habits that grew into hope—real, achievable hope that I might live a new life free of alcohol. At our most primitive level we are motivated to avoid pain. The "want" I talk about throughout this book truly occurs when the pain of continuing to drink is greater than the perceived change in transitioning into sobriety. My recovery represents a unique blending of many aspects of humanity.

I had no idea a football philosophy I learned in the past would someday play a crucial role in me beating my addiction. I had the privilege of playing for one of the winningest high school coaches in Iowa history, Coach Dick Tighe. I also coached with him at St. Edmond High School for eight years. Tighe wrote a short book about his offense in the 1990s: *The No-Frills Power I Belly Offense*. The book outlines philosophical team concepts as well as his top offensive plays. Tighe typically operated with six to ten plays, focusing on quality, not quantity. We repeated the same drills and techniques over and over again. A powerful line in the book reads, "Repetition breeds confidence and confidence equals wins."

Tighe's players didn't have to think too hard on Friday nights—they just had to execute. I was Tighe's disciple, and I tried to replicate his style when I became a head coach. I had no idea this same philosophy would someday play a critical role in my win against alcohol addiction.

Repetition breeds confidence and confidence equals wins.

Repetition and routines are huge in early sobriety and for moving forward. It varies in degree from person to person, but those trying to achieve sobriety have a brain with a stripped-out reward system. Think about it: The only way I'd experienced happiness, laughter, joy, contentment, bliss, etc. was through using alcohol to release dopamine, serotonin, and other neurotransmitters. It was like trying to feel real emotions at a distance. Eventually, with time and persistence, my brain recalibrated and fixed itself to get me to a much better place. Thick skin, tunnel vision, and doing the work over and over again like players in Tighe's offense brought confidence and self-efficacy. *Repetition leads to confidence and confidence leads to wins.*

What did I do each day to carry me through? My perceptions, mental processes, physical activities, and practices became the primary tools in my toolbox. Sobriety and recovery are very personal and somewhat subjective, though in speaking with many others who have battled alcoholism, many common denominators exist. I'm not a medical doctor, so nothing here should be taken as medical advice.

Also, the name of the game here is quitting alcohol, and desperate times call for desperate measures, so I'll suggest eating sugar, processed carbs, and other things that may not necessarily be healthy for you. *I don't care!* If you have to drink Mountain Dew and eat Captain Crunch and gradually wean yourself off that, then so be it.

I was totally addicted and dependent on alcohol; I needed it to function. I highly suggest getting a medical professional involved as you begin your recovery. I needed medical detox to get started. You may too, if you are in a deep state of physical addiction, so take all necessary precautions as you transition into your recovery. As such, this perspective on sobriety and recovery is geared toward those with advanced addictions. Does that mean that it only applies to us?

Absolutely not. Anyone believing that they may have a problem with alcohol or know someone who does can benefit from this story. Bear in mind that some of my suggestions and methods may be scrutinized in that it may lead to other unhealthy addictions, such as sugar. For me, the end justifies the means. If we have to deal with sugar later, so be it. As I've said, we are laser-focused on ridding ourselves of alcohol addiction, may the heavens fall.

Another word of caution: What worked for me may not work for you. As alcohol addicts, we go through most of the same stuff, but I am not you genetically, environmentally, socially, etc. You have to find your natural golf or baseball swing to hit this ball. You will definitely want to research and study as many sobriety and recovery sources as possible to find what truly works for you!

In the Beginning, There Was Little Light (90 Days)

The beginning sucks, plain and simple. Your brain is in crisis mode and it's deploying every signal it can muster to get you to drink alcohol, primarily using a barrage of anxiety. I spent three days in the hospital on benzos, which took the very tip of the spear away, though it took a good three to four weeks before withdrawal symptoms truly began to ease.

This is where you will rely heavily on your *want*—you're going to have to manufacture your own positivity at times, so fake it till you make it. This period is a phase, and it will pass. Around Day 70, I could feel my cognition returning and a feeling of indescribable mental wellness and improvement. It turns out this is fairly common. The next tips were absolutely critical for my early sobriety, so do them:

Recognize the Lies

This is the most important thing to remember: The Black Dog is a highly skilled liar. The bastard uses casuistry to slip you up, but he's lying. His mental tricks are always cons. If you take time to examine some of the thoughts he's preaching, you'll uncover how irrational they are, though they might sound like gospel. Prepare yourself for your hijacked mind to turn on you. It's not its fault: it has been trained, conditioned, and modified for regular alcohol intake. It will heal and recalibrate, and soon serve you well. It's just sick for now. You can kennel his lies and his barking.

Fight, dear child, fight!

Do the Work

It's essential to seek therapy or some version of mental healing as highlighted in chapter 12, or some other method of psychological and emotional healing. The drink is a symptom of an issue within you which must be addressed and healed. There are extremely effective, promising methods utilizing trauma modalities that may work wonders for you. A good sober coach or sponsor can be an extremely beneficial guide.

A word of caution: Be careful when picking at old wounds because they usually contain a lot of pus. Ensure you have the proper support in place to take on this emotional toil.

Build Your Team

Other than the intensive outpatient treatment that left plenty to be desired, I did not attend any groups or meetings to battle my addiction. I'm not bragging or gloating; it just wasn't the right path for me. However, I haven't been fighting this battle in a vacuum. I'm so fortunate to have a wife who stood by my side and supported me, kids that fill my life with joy, and though my social circle has shrunk significantly, I have a handful of great friends. I did much of my sobriety and recovery work on my own, though this loving team fueled me to do the work. The love and support were always there, so I rarely felt unsupported.

Alesha and I had a big social circle. We hosted so many parties: Christmas parties, pool parties, the annual Iowa versus Iowa State football game party. We went on couples trips with friends, went bar hopping, and enjoyed day drinking with most of our social circle.

Alcohol was always at the center of it all. When the news got out about me, we experienced an enormous rush of support. People stopped by. I received various social media reachouts, and people cared about us and the potential impact this might have on our family.

Despite the initial enthusiasm, the circle shrank. I was surprised to learn it didn't bother me too much. I found that other than my wife, children and a few close friends and family members, I didn't really seem to care who stayed in my life. This was a strange epiphany, one of many that would begin a dawn of awakening that would transcend into a new life, one where I would finally find the strength to face Patrick Farley for who he truly was, reach a hand out to him, help him up, and tell him that everything would be okay, and he would actually live, *truly* live.

If you lack a grounded cast of supportive friends and family, I don't suggest going it alone. You'll need support from others, plain and simple. I would strongly encourage AA or some other sober community if you find yourself on an island against the oceanic tug of alcohol.

Set Some Goals

There is no shortage of goal-making processes out there, but I like Strategic, Measurable, Attainable, Realistic, and Timely (SMART) goals. Your number one goal is to stay sober for the day. Take it one day at a time at first. AA is correct here, especially early on, but you can set some bigger goals to get yourself excited. Goals and dreams unlock and create the passion for this new life.

Create Your Routine Plan

You'll need to create a plan for every day. Whether you plan out your day in a planner, notebook, online calendar, it doesn't matter. Find the will to create a daily plan for yourself. We want our routines to become habit-like.

Build Happiness Maps

Visualize and fantasize about where this ride might take you. When you're at the beginning phases of kicking booze, your new life might be hard to visualize, but you're going to go through a metamorphosis very similar to that of a butterfly.

Chart, diagram, scribble, draw, whatever—generate a visual guide of your personal happiness in recovery. Create a *real* bucket list, one that you can accomplish because alcohol won't prevent you from tackling it.

It might be difficult because you may think, "Shit, I can't drink wine when I take my once-in-a-lifetime trip to Italy." But know the absence of alcohol will eventually cease to be a big deal during your alcohol-free progression.

Dream big. I cringe to think that I was spending up to $1,500 per month on alcohol, bars, and restaurants (some food, mostly booze). Now money can go toward investing, saving for something you want, an earlier retirement—you'll likely have more disposable income coming to you soon. Map your inner desires and dream big.

Devise To-Do Lists

Time block, don't time block, whatever works for you. To-do lists differ from routines, though they are linked. Once established, routines become habit-like, operate by way of daily timing, and become somewhat automatic. Structured segments of happenings go into your schedule by mental and physiological conditioning. Completing tasks eases anxiety and provides a small sense of achievement. I'm a checkmark guy; I love to check things off lists I've created for myself.

Before alcohol got the better of me, I was the master of lists. During the mess, I created lists of both possible and impossible tasks, flighty ideas, and things I can't make sense of today. (*What the hell does "roll the boulder toward Jeremy and see if there is fire?" mean?* I don't know anyone named Jeremy, and I'm scared he was involved in a situation with me that involved alcohol, boulders, and fire.)

Needless to say, drunken Pat accomplished little. Even if you only write down two things, write that shit down and check it off!

Drink Water

Water consumption helps our body and brain in every way possible. We all hear this, but seriously. Drinking water throughout the day comes with an ever-present sense of well-being and an overall feeling of being better than okay. I'd been living like a piece of beef jerky for decades, and even before then, I wasn't drinking enough water. Drinking a lot of water helps mood, energy, and gives your body a much-needed daily flush. I drink a gallon a day. Our brains are 80% water, so drink up.

Exercise

Exercise is a huge part of recovery! Whether you have a history of working out or not, you gotta get your body moving. It doesn't need to be boot camp; walking is more than enough. Exercise might be the one thing that best combats anxiety. It also allows you to process your thoughts and emotions.

I got used to listening to several fantastic books and podcasts that discuss addiction. Several have certainly engaged my interest and have been of great help in my journey. They really helped me understand and empathize with others' addictions.

Sleep

Our alcoholic lives have prevented us from getting quality sleep. The amount of damage depends on the time, quantity, and frequency of your consumption. Sleep cycles in stages and hopefully always reaches the rapid eye movement (REM) stage. This is the restorative stage of sleep, where the brain repairs and washes itself. We also dream during this stage. REM suffers terribly with excessive alcohol use. When we begin sleeping without it, the brain goes crazy and says "Yes! No booze, let's get to work on rebuilding!"

This is known as rebound REM, and for some of us, leads to crazy-ass dreams! I believe that many of these dreams have unconscious value and are worth paying attention to.

You may find sleep tough immediately after quitting, but you'll eventually find healing and restoration. Many of us in recovery have come to love the sleep that we earn throughout the day. You might find the hours when you typically used to drink difficult; the Black Dog wanted me to feed him between 5 p.m. and 10 p.m. It, like most other symptoms of alcoholism, fades.

However, by going to bed early, we double down on several benefits: We cut the Black Dog off at the pass, hopefully only enduring its nagging for a few hours per night. We get more sleep and can wake up earlier to seize the day.

Benjamin Franklin was right: "Early to bed, early to rise, makes us healthy, wealthy, and wise."

Sugar

I told you I was going to do it: Your body breaks alcohol into acetate to use as fuel. The body prefers glucose (sugar), and drinking or eating sugar can assuage alcohol cravings. I know, I know, sugar is evil, it's addictive, it causes inflammation.

Beer is actually better for you than soda pop (an argument I was oh, so fond of making while I was drunk Pat). But beer and its affiliates tried to kill me, so I used sugar to get it off my back. I'm not saying go crazy, but if you're looking for relief and the craving has you on the ropes, use sugar.

Pro tip: If you mix all the fruity flavors at a fountain pop station together, it sort of tastes like a mocktail. Some suggest that you can deal with weight gain later. I actually lost fifty pounds, even while taking in a lot of sugar, and have kept it off. The exercise helps balance this. Either way, the name of the game is beating alcohol.

I also gravitated toward breakfast cereal, which is loaded with sugar. Maybe I also liked it because beer and cereal share the same ingredients: wheat, barley, oats, corn, and rice. I don't know. Choose your favorite cereal from when you were a kid to add some childhood nostalgia and go to town. It worked for me.

Non-Alcoholic (NA) Seltzers/Other NA Drinks

I like seltzers, and you can buy a variety of flavors. Plus, they bubble like beer. When my cravings were bad, I'd sneak into my garage and chug one, as I used to do with beer. I scared Alesha more than once when she caught me.

Some may argue, "You're still practicing deception and drinking behavior."

Yep, and don't care. It's not alcohol, and that's more than enough. Plus, the urge to guzzle the seltzer dissipated as my reliance and love of alcohol withered. I have yet to drink a non-alcoholic beer. I don't know that I ever will—it just seems like a bad idea.

Journal

Recording what's on your mind helps you think, process emotions, and generate a history of yourself to study later. You don't have to write a lot, nor do you have to journal every day. It's okay to cycle in and out of journaling. Some days, just a sentence is enough.

I use a whole host of prompts that I assign myself, such as, "What are we scared of today?" Like many things in recovery, the more you do it, the more comfortable you become at finding your groove. Remember, repetition breeds confidence.

Supplements and Medications

Many supplements claim one thing or another, but I tend to stick to the basics: a good multivitamin and quality omega-3 fatty acid supplements. I can tell when I forget to take them, as they help with my energy and mood. I also take anti-anxiety medication, and the side effects have been minimal.

One important word of advice: Work with your doctor to explore and discover the right timing for your medication. I was taking mine in the morning, which I found wasn't ideal, so I switched to taking it before bed, and it made a world of difference. I don't plan to stay on anti-anxiety medication for the rest of my life—I'm actually looking into weaning off it soon, though I wouldn't hesitate to go back on if needed.

Massage Therapy

Massages helped "fix" the dopaminergic release dysfunction in my brain and also eased anxiety. If you like massages, find the style that suits you and enjoy it. They might be a bit pricey, but at a couple hundred bucks once or twice a month, these efforts to help erase your drunken aftereffects are well worth it.

Hot Baths

Especially in the cold months, hot baths are bliss. Soaps, bubble bath, and Epsom salts are all good, but the warm/hot water alone is enough to balm your nervous system.

Pets

I think pets might be the most underrated sobriety asset. Sherman and I are exceptionally close. From the time I stepped into my house after Matt dropped me off, Sherman knew something was terribly wrong. He forced his way onto my lap during dark days and has been by my side ever since. He's my walking buddy and provides me with companionship and unconditional love (sometimes he offers too much affection!) when I was going through the pains of getting sober. If you have a dog or other pet, they'll likely know you're going through a troubled time. Let them help you.

Stress Management

I can't overstate the importance of managing stress. In my case, poor stress management got me into my alcohol problems in the first place. Most of the items included in this segment lend themselves to stress management. It's important to feel and keep a constant radar up for when your body and brain are telling you they're overwhelmed.

Practice breathing, meditation, and finding other ways to self-soothe.

Gratitude

I used to tell the football players in our leadership class to have an "attitude of gratitude." Being grateful for the blessings in your life can change your perspective. It will be hard to come by some days, and I'm not talking about toxic positivity that can degenerate into inauthenticity.

There are many, many people who would kill to have your problems, so find as many little things you can to be grateful for, think about them, journal on them, and keep in mind that the longer you stay in recovery, the more you'll feel grateful for. Scout's honor!

Learn to Reallocate Your Time

I used to be very protective of my time when I was in active alcohol addiction, especially during evenings and weekends. When it was time to drink, it was time to drink! Everything else needed to get out of the way (until I simply started sneaking the drink). I spent so much time drinking that the behavior itself claimed a large swath of time, and I protected it. Once you leave the bottle, your inclination to reserve time for drinking remains.

One day, I was teaching with Brad, an English teacher and an old friend. Brad was an excellent teacher and very wise. I was discussing how I might not go to an event because it was two hours away. Brad replied, "What else are you going to do?"

These seven words were pure gold. When you find yourself reluctant to do things, ensure you're not protecting old drinking time routines. *What else are you going to do?*

Post-Acute Withdrawal Syndrome (PAWS)

Post-Acute Withdrawal Syndrome (PAWS) typically occurs after prolonged and heavy alcohol use. It often includes ongoing fuzziness, disorientation, decreased attention span, befuddled organizational skills, and feeling crummy even after weeks and months of sobriety.

We did a number on our brains, and they need time to heal. Stay the course.

This Sucks . . . Wait, I Think Things are Actually Getting Better! (The Next Six Months)

In March 2024, my family and I flew to visit my dad and Connie, who are now retired in Palm Coast, Florida. I was over ninety days sober and gaining confidence. It was so good to get away from the Iowa winter. However, I was not at all sure how I would handle alcohol triggers on a getaway to Florida. Arriving at the airport in Cedar Rapids and seeing the wonderful lighted bottles of liquor in the bars conveniently located right next to the terminals were enticing, as were the drinks served on the plane. Those cute little mini bottles . . . I realized I had not flown without imbibing since my twenties.

A little voice said (much smaller now), *"Maybe we can . . ."*

"WHO THE HELL LET YOU OUT!? Shut the hell up and go back to your kennel, you gaslighting little bitch," I growled at it.

I didn't know how much of my situation my dad and Connie knew, but I was prepared to unveil the whole story should they inquire.

It never came up.

One of the few times compassion gets extended to you in the Farley family is when life legitimately has you down despite your best efforts. We just don't really talk about it (or if we do, it's brief) and we defend and take the side of the Farley in peril. I have enough people in my corner to process my alcohol troubles, so I was okay not talking to my dad about it.

We went to some spring training baseball games. The Red Sox were playing the Yankees in Tampa Bay at George Steinbrenner field. This was tough because I couldn't take advantage of my favorite beer and baseball combo, but it wasn't as bad as I thought it might be. Soda pop and peanuts carried me through the enormous advertisements for my favorite libations as well as watching folks around me enjoying the seductive Black Dog sauce that had attempted to ruin my life.

But after our trip, I started to have thoughts like, "Holy smokes, this thing does go away," and, "I may be able to take this on after all."

Here were my observations six to nine months in:

Expectations Can Be Preconceived Resentments

In March 2024, I took Alesha and the kids to a Red Sox spring training game in Tampa Bay, Florida Red Sox vs. Yankees. It was my first Major League Baseball game, and more than that, my first real outing sober. I'd been looking forward to it for weeks. The idea of sharing that experience with my family, of being present and clear-headed, felt like a milestone, a kind of victory lap for the work I'd been doing in recovery.

The stadium buzzed with energy, sunlight bouncing off jerseys, the crack of the bat echoing through the crowd, vendors shouting over the hum of anticipation. It was everything I'd imagined. But as the game unfolded, I found myself wrestling with a quiet truth: without booze, the experience felt . . . different. Not worse, just unfamiliar. The old version of me would've had a beer in hand, maybe two or ten, letting the alcohol smooth out the edges of social anxiety or amplify the excitement. This time, I was raw. Present. A little off-balance.

I still had fun, laughing with the kids, soaking in the rivalry, watching Alesha light up when the Sox scored. But it was at that game, in the middle of the seventh inning stretch, that I learned something important: expectations need to be tempered. Sobriety doesn't guarantee joy in every moment. It offers clarity, and sometimes that clarity reveals discomfort, awkwardness, or unmet hopes. That's part of the deal.

Looking back, I wouldn't trade that day for anything. It marked a shift and a realization that we must learn to expect a different brand of joy and contentment, something authentic and real.

Nothing is more true when recovering from alcohol addiction. While hooked, we all look forward to the next opportunity to drink. We expect to have fun with alcohol at home, at concerts, garages, bars, restaurants, sporting events, wineries, in our cars. We quickly guzzle when no one is looking (at social events, before church, at work in a school—I'm not the only one!). We learn that alcohol is the height of fun and enjoyment and we expect it to be at the center of everything, especially vacations and outings. These expectations remain after quitting alcohol, but if we expect the same boozy feeling to accompany life events while being alcohol free, we face terrible disappointment.

That's not to say life simply sucks after alcohol. It doesn't, trust me! However, you must temper your expectations, especially as you begin to reexperience things sober. It will not be the same, but with time spent sober, you build new neural pathways to enjoy life without alcohol.

Prepare to Be Misunderstood

Alcohol has a grip on society. You'll now be outside the social norm, especially in many of the circles we run in and the things we do for fun. Some people will understand, some won't care, some will judge you harshly for escaping the cave. Do your best to stay true to yourself and allow the battery and the alternator to continue to generate energy and excitement for this new life.

Know You Can Relearn

You learned many, many behaviors and thinking patterns under the influence. Socializing, connecting with people, dancing, etc. all often occur while drinking. You'll feel a sense of emptiness when trying to reengage with these things. You learned them while drinking and they have been reinforced over time often while drinking. It takes time, but as your brain repairs itself and regains a solid sober consciousness, you will realize that you are fully capable of doing the things you once did (if you still want to do them!) using the lab in your brain to naturally generate a new chemical cocktail.

Fatigue and Brain Fog, Biological Rhythms and Cycles

Early on, you'll feel tired all the time, and your memory and cognition will feel slow and fuzzy. Your brain is repairing itself, but it will eventually self-correct. Rely on time and persistence, and the fog and tiredness will clear.

We operate within a realm of certain biological timing mechanisms. The sun creates our circadian cycle, or rhythm of twenty-four hour days. We also have twenty-eight to thirty day cycles, ninety-day cycles, and 365-day (yearly) cycles. Think of it as an enormous clock with different-sized gears turning at different speeds, determining when to release hormones, adjust internal temperatures, downshift energy exertion, and sadly, when to expect surplus alcohol. After decades of heavy drinking, the Black Dog penetrates this system as well.

I did my heaviest drinking at certain times and on certain days. Cravings hit hard then, like being underwater and needing air. These are what the craving felt like. Literally, they seemed as physiological as the need for air. It was terrible, though these cravings were later reduced to mental longings. Some happened because of social cues, though this biological timing mechanism also learned when it was time to drink. Sundays, birthdays, Christmas, Father's Day, Fourth of July, etc. are particularly triggering, though as the days in recovery go by, our timing gears get fixed and stop firing drinking impulses on these days and times. This is not to say you won't have urges to drink later, but the longer you stay out of the bottle, the more your brain will extinguish these once-prominent drunken cycle dates.

Anhedonia

My brian relied on alcohol to gain unearned dopamine. Now, without it, and especially in early sobriety, dopamine is low. Low dopamine is a key symptom of depression, a prolonged period of severe boredom and loss of interest, and a seeming inability to feel pleasure. Anhedonia is a psychological condition in which someone loses the ability to feel pleasure from activities they once enjoyed. It feels as though life has a constant dullness. This is why it is so important to do your best to exercise, create happiness maps, to-do lists, and goals. These brought me hope as I battled. You will need to replace your old drinking lifestyle with new pastimes and joys as your brain heals itself and these symptoms decrease. Your healing brain and your new life will see you through.

Beware Replacement Addictions but Keep the Goodie Bag Handy

What the hell, Pat? You said to eat sugar!

Yes, and certainly in early sobriety, though it's probably something you should wean yourself off later. Your brain seeks to be as efficient as possible, so it may link what used to be an addiction to alcohol to food, shopping, overspending money, unhealthy sexual avenues, or other addictions. You don't want to take on a new addiction battle down the road.

And yet, I still say, much the same way you used to cart booze clandestinely, you might consider toting a grab bag of goodies filled with candy, fruit, nuts, jerky; whatever floats your boat. Should a craving hit, access the goodie bag.

Sex

Sobriety circles don't often discuss sex. It's a bit taboo, and it presents complications for many as it relates to their addictions. My sex drive was nonexistent for months in early sobriety. As I became more comfortable with my recovery and as exercise, nutrition and overall wellness progressed, my libido resurfaced, letting me know it's alive and well.

Sex is a need, and it offers a source of connection and pleasure for many.

Sober sex is often great sex, and I am very much glad to be back in the game. Be sure that you are emotionally, physically, and relationally ready to be intimate. If so, take advantage of it—it's one of the biggest benefits of being alcohol free.

Movies, Streaming, and Shows

I'm a movie junkie. As alcohol took control of my life, I watched a lot of TV while drinking. In early sobriety, I thought I had lost my love for it. But now that I'm sober, I nearly pee with excitement when I can squeeze them in, though I've had to rewatch many, many of my favorites so I know how they end.

Identity Work

When we quit drinking, we must also quit our "drinking identity." However, it's a big part of socializing and becomes interwoven into our personality. Friends and even family members may not understand this, so clarifying your identity is huge. Find out for yourself who you want to be and perhaps you might get there. You are very much like a butterfly in a cocoon: You have taken on a massive life change. This takes some serious looking inside and introspective work. Be sure your regeneration is being crafted and developed by you toward your very own self-actualization.

Prioritize Recovery

Nothing should be more important to you than your recovery. I get it, life is busy, but if you don't make time to generate a plan to keep your recovery alternator returning a charge, you risk relapse. You've come too far for that. It's not selfish, it's literally your life.

Understand You're Different

Everyone has to deal with crap in their lives. This is just our thing, our cross to bear. When I go into a restaurant, I still look to see what kind of whiskey they have. I scan the room to see who's having a drink. Normal drinkers (and certainly abstainers) don't do this. It's weird. Our relationship with alcohol is different, and we must cope with and manage it.

Timing

The book *When* by Daniel Pink explains timing in great and very interesting detail as it applies to our own neurochemistry and how it relates to success. So much of *how* we feel and *when* we feel it operates in predictable patterns. Syncing this timing with when to work out, eat, sleep, plan for big events, etc. can help us accomplish the things we want to get done, especially as it applies to our mood and energy levels. If we coordinate our behaviors within the confines of our peaks in performance, success is at our fingertips.

Carve Out a Sober Spot

Where is the best place to think, reflect, write, or feel? Find your own corner of the universe where you can think, where you can be you and work on the *you* you strive to be. It can be an office, a sitting area, a workout space—whatever feels good.

One Year and Beyond: I'm Back, Baby! (Kind of)

Life without alcohol is . . . different.

At some point, the alcohol stopped working. In a downward recession cycle, everything about who I was and how I felt declined. Over time, the boosts became smaller and less impacting. The buzz didn't work. Drunkenness didn't work. Impairment and passing out was all that was left.

Our brains have a naturally occurring thought process that can knock the socks off of any substance when it comes to mood, energy, and being our best selves: true happiness. We need only to learn how to tap into it. Today, mine is in full throttle and I feel better at a regular baseline mood than I ever did under alcohol's spell.

The Brain Self-Corrects: Biological Recalibration

"The mind is beautiful because of the paradox. It uses itself to understand itself."

—Adam Elenbaas

The human brain is the most complicated mechanism on the planet. The brain is extremely interconnected. Every part does a little of everything, though there are regions largely responsible for certain functions. I know you know I'm headed for a brain science lesson (I have the heart of a teacher! *What did you expect?*) but even though I'm a brain science geek, I'll try to keep this section as interesting as possible.

There are more connections in the brain than there are stars in the universe. Fortunately, it's also adaptive and possesses the ability to heal itself to a certain extent. Neuroplasticity allows it to modify, learn, change, and regenerate to accommodate the demands of our lives. Our brains want us to be happy and physically well, but it also seeks predictability and familiarity. It constantly takes input through the senses to act accordingly.

Sadly, many of us have flooded it with alcohol over time and it has learned a lot of the wrong things. The key areas of the brain involved in addiction:

- **Nucleus accumbens (NAc):** The human brain has evolved over many years, and has done so from the lower portion up. Think of the foundation of a house, starting with the basement and building to the first floor on up. Above the brain stem, which handles automatic functions such as breathing and blood pressure, lives the limbic system, which handles emotion, memory, and motivation. The NAc, which administers a mesolimbic dopamine system, is attached to the limbic system. The NAc is a reward system that primarily delivers pleasure anticipation and creates cravings.
- **Prefrontal cortex or frontal lobes:** When you look at a picture of a brain, you probably see a noodle-like tube all smashed together in a weird oval shape. This noodle tube sits atop the rest of the brain. It's the most evolved component, called the cortex, and it's segmented into different lobes. Right behind our foreheads lies the prefrontal cortex—the boss of the brain. It's in charge of the executive functioning that makes us truly human. Creativity, decision making, judgments, thought-induced behavior: all of it comes from the frontal lobes.

- **Amygdala:** This is a small almond-shaped gland that regulates our fight-flight emotions, stress hormones, and sends cue-induced craving signals. It makes us feel as if we're going to get eaten by a lion if we don't mainline booze.
- **Hippocampus:** Memory lives everywhere in the brain, though this region is largely responsible for coordination and muscle memory. Memories of past drinking experiences create habit loops, or automatic conditioned responses.

If you're addicted to alcohol, you've successfully messed up all of these brain functions. Congratulations! They're FUBAR. When we develop addictions, we've essentially trained these brain components to adjust their functions, to modify themselves to accommodate and depend on alcohol. But with time, exercise, water, and all the self-care stuff, the brain's neuroplastic features will repair and rewire. You'll be you again—you'll see.

If you've ever gotten a tooth extracted, you know the experience is not pleasant. There's the healing pain, the fear that the clot will not form correctly and lead to a dry socket, and then, your tongue doesn't recognize the new demographic of its home. That's similar to what's happening in your brain when you leave alcohol addiction. The body has to get to know itself all over again.

As this chapter comes to a close, I want to leave you with a warning about a thinking pattern I've wrestled with and still do from time to time if I'm not careful: It's the fear of maintaining sobriety *forever*. That daunting word—*FOREVER!*—can take the wind out of your sails. *Will I ever have fun again? Will I ever feel joy? Is sober life just endless dullness?*

Here's the truth: You can't see it now, and that's the problem, because the energy, effort, and sacrifice you're putting into early sobriety doesn't represent what your recovery mindset will become.

It gets easier. So much easier. As the fine folks in AA preach, no one is saying you can never drink again, you're just not going to drink today.

As your brain heals and new habits take hold, joy begins to return, and with it, clarity, laughter, and peace. Some days, "one day at a time" is the only mantra that makes sense. And on those days, the folks in AA got it exactly right. My own mindset still shifts back and forth. Sometimes I'm locked into long-term purpose and gratitude. Other days, I just need to get through the next twenty-four hours, and both are okay. Both mindsets are valid and part of recovery.

I've always loved fall. The changing leaves, the cool air, the scent of earth and wood smoke is always magical. But in my old life, alcohol was tied to that magic. My first autumn in sobriety was tough. I couldn't enjoy the beauty. I couldn't *feel* it. The season arrived, but I couldn't receive it.

A year later? The magic grew a little more, and I can't wait for this coming fall.

Time heals wounds, including the ones carved by addiction. Stick with it. Trust the process. The joy you think you've lost is not gone—it's just waiting for the fog to lift.

Now, go back in time with me for a bit.

Sunday, July 6, 2025: A Day in Recovery

I wake on my own and glance at the clock: 5:46 a.m. It's early, but the quiet feels perfect. The flannel comforter is cozy against my skin, and I burrow in for a few more moments. Alesha's still asleep beside me. I give her a soft kiss on the cheek and ease out of bed.

Stretching tall, I lift the blinds just enough to peek out at the neighborhood from the second floor. The lawn, freshly mowed yesterday, glows green in the morning light. Potted petunias bloom from clay pots around the house, and a cardinal hops near the wood stack. It's peaceful, still carrying remnants of Friday's Fourth of July celebrations. Spent fireworks cartridges and cardboard litter the driveways and curbs.

It's Sunday. No work today. I grab a T-shirt and shorts without overthinking what I'll wear.

Most of my clothes are either too big or just right now—one of the quiet gifts of sobriety. As I make my way downstairs, sunlight filters through the west-facing window, dancing on the leaves outside. Another steamy Iowa day—thank goodness for air conditioning.

The kids—Boston, Tessi, and Chelsey—are already in the living room, energetically demanding waffles. I pull out my trusty thirty-year-old waffle maker (still spinning like a champ!) and get to work. But first: coffee. On weekends, we break out the grinder and brew the "good stuff," as Cakes calls it. Alesha comes down, pours a mug, and gives me a warm hug and a quick peck. Neither of us has brushed our teeth yet, so we keep it clean.

I whip up a batch of batter and cook about thirty waffles—Boston alone will probably devour ten. Leftovers make for quick weekday breakfasts. Sherman, his tail wagging, cozies up to me, fully aware that affection raises his odds of snagging a waffle.

After breakfast, I glance at my shopping list:

- Dog food
- New radiator cap for the Camry
- Steaks for dinner

I map out the stores I need to hit and estimate the costs. But first: a walk with Sherman. It's our weekend ritual. I avoid using the word "walk" until I'm geared up—Sherman knows it too well and will lose his mind at the mention. I grab my AirPods, phone, and shoes. Today feels like a half-podcast, half-Blink 182 kind of day.

Once ready, I drop the "WALK" bomb and we're out the door. The morning is muggy but not yet oppressively hot. Everything's dewy and lush. Queen Anne's lace blooms along the path, my mom's favorite summer bloom. We dodge firework debris on the way to the trail. Across the red bridge over the creek and into the thicket, the pine trees stand tall and serene. We spot a fox, and Sherman pulls forward on the leash, his little body rigid. He's ready to chase.

"Easy, killer," I laugh.

After our two-mile loop, Sherman jumps into the car and we head to town. The Camry starts without fuss and blasts cold AC—it's bliss. I haven't always had reliable cars, so this feels like luxury.

We grab dog food, then stop by the butcher. Sirloins are reasonable, but the porterhouses look divine. "Five big porterhouses, my good man!" I say with a grin. The butcher smiles and wraps them up.

I nearly forget—we need toilet paper. I grab the jumbo pack. One last stop: the parts store for the radiator cap. The guy behind the counter tosses it to me with a friendly smirk. We've grown more familiar this past year.

That's small-town Iowa for you: community, connection, folks knowing your name.

We're home by noon, just in time for the Red Sox game. Erik, my best friend, arrives, ready to razz the players and cackle at every misstep. We laugh until our stomachs hurt. The game wraps around 3 p.m., and I head to the grill. Alesha's working on potatoes and a fresh salad. The porterhouses sizzle with flavor as they sear. The smell alone is worth the wait.

We all sit down together for dinner. It's calm, real, and filling—in every sense of the word.

Afterward, Erik heads out. I feel another walk coming on. The dips low as Sherman and I gear up again for a short walk as dusk lays its soft fingers across the sky. At home, I settle in and watch The Crown. My eyes grow heavy by 8:30. I say my goodnights and slip into bed, full, tired, and without a single worry in the world.

What the hell, Pat? Did you really just waste five minutes describing an ordinary, boring day?

Not so fast, Batman . . . We'll dissect as to why a day such as this represents miracles in the next chapter.

Chapter 15

After the Storm

"We have two lives, and the second one begins when we realize we only have one."

—Confucious

Upon this book's release, I have secured two years in recovery. Three years ago, never in my wildest dreams would I have thought I could have a life without alcohol. I can say this with certainty, and it's an indescribable feeling: **I don't need a drink.**

I don't need one when I'm stressed. Not when I'm anxious. Not when I'm happy, calm, or at peace. Now, there are times when I kind of would like one. But, I can handle "kind of like one" all day long. It's the need that simply isn't there for now. But let me be clear, I don't believe I'm "cured." I still see the bottles at bars because I instantly glance at them. I still scan the room to see who's drinking and what they have. Occasionally, the thought of drinking "someday" will enter, a clever tactic by the Black Dog, who's always probing, maneuvering, waiting . . .

This is a lifelong journey, one that demands daily intention. I've intensely studied how quickly addiction can roar back if I lower my guard (because the Black Dog wanted me to research if those with alcohol addiction can drink again someday and I did. He's a bugger!)

The empirical answer is: *No, never, please don't. You'll throw away everything very quickly if you do. Addiction-forged neural pathways await this and will be more than happy to take your happy ass right back to where you were in record time.*

Still, as I release this book, my recovery is the most important achievement and next to my family, the first priority in my life. As I surpass my second year in recovery and beyond, my key goal is simple but profound: to sort through the wreckage and the remnants. To discern what remains and what was necessarily swept away by the storm. Recovery isn't just about abstaining, as we've discussed, it's more than sobriety. It's about reckoning. About standing in the quiet aftermath and asking the hardest question of all: *Who am I now? What is my purpose?*

Some parts of me survived intact. Others were stripped away, not out of cruelty, but necessity. The storm brought carnage, though it also revealed. It peeled back the layers of performance, denial, and distraction, leaving behind something raw, something real. Now, I'm committed to the slow work of further analysis. Of allowing time to do its sacred work. Of searching, not for perfection or certainty, neither of these are obtainable, but perhaps I can find my all-too-elusive truth. I seek alignment, meaning, and authenticity. I'm learning to honor the fragments that remain: the teacher, the coach, the man. I'm also learning to grieve what's gone without rushing to replace it. Because this life, this sober, intentional life isn't about rebuilding the old structure. It's about constructing something new from the foundation up. And that starts with knowing who I truly am. My soul has grown old, like a tree that's weathered every season and still reaches for the sun.

Now, this is probably where I'm supposed to say my life is so amazing. That everything is perfect now. That sobriety solved all my problems. But here's the truth: it didn't. **Nothing** solves all of life's problems and difficult challenges. For many of us, alcohol masked the deeper struggles, the things inside us we didn't know how to face. Recovery means meeting those things head-on. It takes time. It takes work.

In my descent into the ugliness of early sobriety, I gradually lost who I was. I couldn't just put a tag on the good parts of me, say "save for later" and toss out the rest. I wish it were that easy. The emptiness of our old persona must be hollowed out because it's where the Black Dog used to live. You have to be willing and want to change. I believe those who truly commit to personal transformation in recovery give themselves a far greater chance of living a life free from alcohol.

I still have hard days. My world is busy, with teenagers in multiple sports, work, and countless moving parts. But if addiction feels like death by a thousand cuts, recovery is the slow, beautiful healing of each one. It's finding fleeting joy, quiet peace, and steady strength in a life no longer ruled by those wounds.

This newfound vigor for living can't be overstated. I built and nurtured these motivations into routines and systems of recovery. I slowly glued together many fragments and pieces. I can now live and peacefully chase that which continues to elude.

Let's go back to July 6 and take a closer look. As a fairly normal weekend day for my family, it may look largely unremarkable to many, but for those of us who have gone through the hell of losing ourselves to alcohol, being able to live and enjoy life without alcohol feels like heaven. To me, these details are remarkable:

1. I could grab whatever T-shirt I wanted. I didn't have to be selective. I wasn't bloated from chugging beer and scarfing down chicken wings all the time. Who knew it'd shrink my waistline that much?

2. I got eight to nine hours of fantastic, sober sleep. Beautiful, restful, rejuvenating sleep. I woke up full of energy and in an excellent mood. If you are in an active addiction, wait

until you get to experience real sleep again. *Amazing.*

3. Sober Sunday sex with a woman I love. I'll leave it at that!

4. Coffee. I couldn't drink coffee while in active addiction. My stomach couldn't tolerate it and it tasted putrid.

5. No hangover, no craving or scheming how to get a drink. Not dehydrated, not throwing up. Priceless.

6. I made a real breakfast for the kids, something I did regularly when they were young but which had all but stopped while actively addicted to alcohol.

7. I enjoyed seeing things and saw beauty in them: Nature, the trees, the yard, birds.

8. I read a chapter of a book. I had all but stopped reading for leisure.

9. I hugged and kissed Alesha with nothing to fear but my bad morning breath. There is no more alcohol on my breath.

10. Alesha came downstairs and smiled. I didn't see much smiling from her when I was drinking. She's happy, and I'm grateful.

11. I walked my dog and simply enjoyed the experience. I earned my dopamine.

12. I listened to music and did not drink alcohol to enjoy it. I had abandoned music while sober.

13. I was knocking out and etching those lovely checkmarks onto my to-do list.

14. I took on a great part-time work opportunity as a crisis mental health counselor and I love it (and the extra money!).

15. I'm grateful for so many things, big and small, from cars that start to AC that blows cold air.

16. I was able to watch a baseball game with a dear friend, and laugh, heckle, and bask in a Red Sox win stone sober.

17. I enjoyed the grilling process and the wonderful porterhouse steak taste. I didn't have to delay eating dinner to protect my buzz. In the past, grilling became a beer-drinking activity. Now, I get to actually enjoy grilling.

18. I was able to purchase the more expensive steak cuts now that I wasn't spending frivolously to mainline booze.

19. My memory is back. I remembered toilet paper unprompted. The big package, too!

20. The auto parts guy is a buddy, not an annoyance. While drinking, I often treated people like crap.

21. There was zero risk of an alcohol-related accident, hurting someone, or an OWI as I did errands.

22. There were no Sunday scaries. My work life is balanced, and I would not have to face my dreaded drunken self or symptoms in the morning.

23. I eased into early stages of sleep naturally and drifted off to better sleep.

24. I didn't have to lie, maneuver, or manipulate anyone in any way. I didn't have to cheat my loved ones.

My list is a simple snapshot, but it barely scratches the surface. There are likely dozens—maybe hundreds—of smaller, subtle joys in one day that come with living sober, things so easily missed while in the throes of alcoholism. These joys now shine with a kind of quiet brilliance. **Life feels real again.** I have my life back. After losing pieces of myself over a thirty-year stretch and utterly spiraling during three of those years, I've regained possession of my soul. And that's not poetic exaggeration; it's the purest, most profound happiness I've ever known.

Medically, I've made a full recovery. My bloodwork is solid. Blood pressure: normal. Liver: regenerated itself like a boss. Every marker that once signaled damage now reflects resilience. But behind those numbers is a deeper truth, because if not for this journey, if not for the decision to fight, there's every reason to believe I wouldn't be here to get the gold star from my doctor. The data confirms what I already know: I survived and I'm coming back stronger. Every breath is evidence of that.

I'm a far better husband now than I ever was before: steadier, softer, and more present in the ways that matter. Yet, when I look back at the loyalty and grace Alesha offered me during the hardest stretches, I feel something deeper than gratitude. I feel undeserving. She stood by me when the road bent sharply, when the light was dim, when I wasn't easy to love. Her support wasn't loud, it was consistent. Unshaken. She believed in a version of me I hadn't yet found. And now, in recovery, I carry that love with reverence. I love her not just as my wife, but as the anchor who reminded me who I could become.

And the kids! Tessi, once more reserved and standoffish, now wraps me in hugs and chatters away, filling rooms with her voice and warmth. Boston, a young man of few words, doesn't speak much, but these days, his laughter and quiet smiles say enough. We're healing together, and Christmas is back, baby! No booze required.

Recovery was never about cutting people out, but alcohol is a powerful thickener of social life. It stitches people together in shared rituals, blurred nights, and inside jokes that sometimes only make sense with a buzz. When sobriety entered the picture, the ones who stayed—who stood with me, not behind the drink—showed their true friendship. Erik still drinks, but makes a conscious effort to keep our friendship strong without it—even back when I wasn't exactly fun to be around in those early recovery days. That effort means everything. Our connection has evolved, but it's still rooted in loyalty and love.

There were moments, while drinking, that felt pure, with genuine laughter, joy, connection. I've tried to recreate those moments sober, and while the results vary, here's what I've learned: Once you experience an old outing through a sober lens, it kicks down the door for new joy. You realize the magic wasn't in the drink, it was in the people, in the shared experience. It doesn't always feel like it, but trust me, eventually there is a recapture of joy.

I still meet up with Joel and Tanielle, my old college roommates, for football games. I catch up with Audel over lunch or dinner. These relationships, preserved by mutual respect and care, remind me that true connection doesn't need alcohol to survive.

Two weeks ago, I was on a mental health crisis call in Iowa Falls, about thirty miles from home. We stabilized the situation, which is always rewarding. There's something uniquely fulfilling about helping people in their darkest moments and seeing the light slowly return.

On my way back, I remembered we were running low on milk. And given Boston's impressive consumption habits, picking up just one gallon wouldn't cut it. Honestly, the kid drinks so much milk it'd probably be more cost-effective to buy a dairy cow and set up shop in the backyard, though I suspect the city wouldn't love that plan.

So there I was, walking out of the store with four gallons of milk in my arms, when a guy in dusty jeans and a short-sleeved button-up—likely a local farmer—looked me up and down as he stood next to his heavy-duty Ford. He smiled and called out, "Looks like you got plenty of milk for the grandkids!"

I gave him a polite smile and nodded, but as I climbed back into my car, I thought, *"What the hell? Does he think I'm Arthur from* The King of Queens? *I'm not a grandpa!"* Then it sank in—I'm forty-seven. Grandparent territory isn't far away. *Holy hell.*

The moment stuck with me, not because of the milk or the comment, but because it made me think. Drinking used to make me feel younger. Alcohol might be the best social lure to convince ourselves that we're still young and vibrant. For so many, booze serves as a kind of collective defense mechanism against aging. If we're still partying like college kids, still tossing back drinks like we used to, then we must still be young, right?

Wrong. That illusion kept me tethered to a version of myself that no longer served me. An elaborate, chemically induced case of Peter Pan syndrome. I'm glad I've stepped out of that delusion. These days, I'm not trying to outrun death or my age, I'm learning to appreciate it. *No beer needed, just old AF.*

Happiness is a deliberate practice. Small decisions and things we do every day can bring us enjoyment and contentment, and this has truly been my recipe for recovery. The now sickly Black Dog will whimper from time to time, but each sober day is a reclamation, a vote for the man I choose to be. Every quiet and often intentional step forward is enough.

Will I ever go back to education? It's a deep question, one that doesn't lend itself to quick answers or easy optimism. Part of me feels that my career in education has run its course. That chapter, with all its twenty-three years of triumphs and failures, may have closed. And yet, another part of me still clings to the idea of standing in front of a classroom again or being the heart of a school. I remember the spark, the way a room could come alive when learning was real, when connection was honest, when purpose was shared. That part of me hasn't died. It has just quieted.

There will forever be a blemish on my teaching credentials. Some will see it as a mark of shame, a disqualifier. Others, fewer perhaps, will recognize it as a scar earned in the battle for reinvention and recovery. The truth is, stigma lingers. And in the world of education, where trust and image are currency, the cost to administrative credibility is real. Hiring someone like me requires courage, vision, and a willingness to see beyond the surface. Not just anyone will do that; they wouldn't want the headaches from the public. I suppose I wouldn't either. But time is a great thickener of things. It settles the dust, softens the edges, and sometimes if we're lucky, may recast the narrative.

So I don't know if I'll return to education in the traditional sense. But I do know this: the impulse to teach, to guide, to build something meaningful is still alive in me. Whether it's through counseling, writing, or community work, the educator in me isn't gone. It just sort of feels like an evolution of some type is taking place. I don't really know the way forward, but I can feel it if that makes any sense.

When I slow the car as I pass the high school, the building holds so many of my life chapters. I walked those halls as a teenager once, full of questions and momentum. Years later, I returned in a suit, charged with leading others through their own seasons of uncertainty. And now, I pass by as a father, watching my children enter that same building each morning with backpacks, AirPods, and futures just beginning to take shape. This school is theirs now. Watching them walk through those same doors fills me with a quiet pride. They don't carry my past, they carry their own possibilities.

At the very moment I should have been standing tall in my career, with my children entering high school, I was instead brought low by my addiction. It felt like a bombshell that shattered not only my professional life but my vision of fatherhood. It has taken time, but today I feel no bitterness about not being inside that school, pulling open office doors, greeting students by name, or offering second chances over coffee-stained desk calendars. There is now a strange sense of gratitude. That school saw me grow, stumble, and rebuild twice, first as a student, later as a principal. It gave me purpose once, and now it gives my children theirs.

I don't work there anymore, but my legacy isn't lost. It lives in the students I supported, in the lessons I taught, and now, in the family I've raised. As I ease the car forward and glance once more in the rearview mirror, I smile. My story with this school isn't over, it has just taken a new form.

What began in a high school office has transformed into something bigger, a mission to speak boldly about recovery, to shine light on the realities of alcohol addiction, and to make space for the underdogs who deserve understanding rather than judgment and scorn. I may no longer hold the title of principal, but I carry forward the same heart: one that stands up for kids who stumble, adults who rebuild, and anyone told they "weren't enough."

We are not unprincipled, low, or without virtue. We went along with the crowd, and in many ways, our addiction chose us as much as we chose it. This thing is real. Call it a disease, disorder, adaptation, whichever you choose. It's real, it grabs us and won't let go. People need to know that we can face and defeat this monster of addiction. We can face the world and say: *This happened. I lived through it. I'm still here.*

The next phase of my life will be rooted less in education, and more so in advocacy, outreach, and direct impact, with joy, purpose, and determination guiding each step. If the world needs someone to hold up a mirror and say, "You can come back from this," then I'm ready to be that voice. The best is absolutely still to come. I'm not the same person that I was that fateful day in December. And in the end, that's what this storm has been all about. My work is far from done.

Epilogue

Contrary to the wisdom of Bob Marley, for decades, there was a constant sense that everything little thing was definitely not going to be all right. That has lifted, and it is such a weight to be relieved of. Optimism and a feeling of no longer being trapped prevails. The notion is indescribable, light and freeing. Success has also taken on a different face to me.

I used to measure success in course syllabi, GPAs, scholarships, and year-end teacher evaluations. In those days, my worth felt tied to a high school building. I ended up trading that for polished lecture halls and the quiet prestige of higher education. Iowa State University took a chance on me in February 2024, while I was still battling through sobriety. When I joined Iowa State University's Ivy College of Business as a recruitment coordinator and adjunct professor, I gained exactly what I thought I needed: title, stability, confidence. It reassured me I could still belong in a professional space, that I hadn't lost my edge.

But something essential was missing. Despite the prestigious environment, I felt an unmistakable pull to return to the front lines, the raw, unfiltered kind of teaching that doesn't revolve around rubrics or academic pedigree. I missed connecting with students whose lives didn't fit neatly into transcripts. I missed the challenge, the discomfort, and the profound honor of showing up for youth who hadn't been given much support at all. I wanted to go back to the start.

When the Iowa Board of Educational Examiners ruled on a deferred suspension, I held my breath. The outcome was redemptive, my licenses remained valid. And with that, I walked into the State Training School in Eldora, Iowa. I began teaching English face-to-face with adjudicated youth, they call them the "the worst of the worst." I was back to teaching kids whose stories were often misunderstood or ignored. I was back where I felt comfortable. In that classroom, transformation didn't come with gold stars. It came through presence. Through listening. Through showing up consistently for students who had never had an adult simply sit and listen to them.

I was afraid that alcohol had stolen my skill set to reach kids, but no. It was still there. There were tough days, though I could still develop all-important relationships with these young men. I challenged them to read, driven by their natural curiosity, and I taught them that writing is the most important and powerful thing they can do for themselves.

This work has always filled my bucket in ways prestige never could. These kids, rough around the edges, brilliant in their own ways, reminded me why I became an educator in the first place. I keep in touch with the ones who have been discharged. I speak with one of my favorites, Omarion, most weeks, over lunch. He'll be completing a degree soon, now having a potential future ahead that previously he couldn't fathom. I'm convinced I was put on the planet to witness successes like his.

I currently serve with Iowa Workforce Development as an advisor, helping underserved parents and veterans find meaningful employment. It has more than simply a new job; it provided much-needed restoration. I bring the full weight of my experience to the work: the theory and research that grounded me, the grit that shaped me, the heartbreak that taught me, and the empathy that saved me.

I also work part-time with UnityPoint as a mental health crisis counselor, responding to individuals when they're most vulnerable. It's where my strength meets compassion and where empathy becomes action.

In the quiet margins of my schedule, I volunteer as a sobriety coach, walking one-on-one with people facing the same battle I once chose to fight. My fight continues and in this role I genuinely feel my humanity. I don't lead from a podium, I sit beside them, shoulder to shoulder, heart to heart.

My career didn't climb in the traditional sense, it shifted. It bent toward healing, advocacy, truth, and hope. And in that shift, I discovered the teacher I had always been trying to become: one who teaches by showing up, by listening, by surviving, and by helping others do the same.

To contact the author for information regarding presentations, public speaking engagements, or if you are interested in one-on-one recovery coaching services, please email unprincipledrecovery@gmail.com

Sources

Alcoholics Anonymous. (2002). *Alcoholics Anonymous: The story of how many thousands of men and women have recovered from alcoholism* (4th ed.). Alcoholics Anonymous World Services.

Amen, D. G. (2020). *The end of mental illness: How neuroscience is transforming psychiatry and helping prevent or reverse mood and anxiety disorders, ADHD, addictions, PTSD, psychosis, personality disorders, and more.* Carol Stream, IL: Tyndale Momentum.

Freud, S. (2015). *Beyond the pleasure principle.* Mineola, NY: Dover Publications. (Original work published 1920)

Freud, S. (1955). *The interpretation of dreams* (J. Strachey, Trans.). New York, NY: Basic Books. (Original work published 1900)

Frankl, V. E. (2006). *Man's search for meaning.* Boston, MA: Beacon Press. (Original work published 1946)

Jung, C. G. (1969). *The archetypes and the collective unconscious* (R. F. C. Hull, Trans., 2nd ed., Vol. 9, Part 1). Princeton, NJ: Princeton University Press. (Original work published 1936)

Kandel, E. R., Koester, J. D., Mack, S. H., & Siegelbaum, S. A. (2021). *Principles of neural science* (5th ed.). New York, NY: McGraw-Hill Education.

McKowen, L. (2020). *We are the luckiest:* The surprising magic of a sober life. New World Library.

Nietzsche, F. (1969). *Thus spoke Zarathustra: A book for everyone and no one* (R. J. Hollingdale, Trans.). London: Penguin Books. (Original work published 1883–1885)

Pascal, B. (1995). *Pensées* (A. J. Krailsheimer, Trans.). London: Penguin Classics. (Original work published 1670)

Pink, D. H. (2018). *When: The scientific secrets of perfect timing*. New York, NY: Riverhead Books.

Plato. (1992). *Republic* (G. M. A. Grube, Trans., rev. C. D. C. Reeve). Indianapolis, IN: Hackett Publishing. (Original work published ca. 380 BCE)

Sartre, J.-P. (2003). *Being and nothingness* (H. E. Barnes, Trans.; 2nd ed.). London: Routledge. (Original work published 1943)

Sartre, J.-P. (2007). *Existentialism is a humanism* (C. Macomber, Trans.). New Haven, CT: Yale University Press. (Original work published 1946)

www.ingramcontent.com/pod-product-compliance
Lightning Source LLC
Chambersburg PA
CBHW070909130626
46555CB00001B/62